STUDY GUIDE on PRIESTLEY'S

AN INSPECTOR CALLS

MADE SUPER SUPER EASY

TEXT EXPLAINED IN GREAT DETAIL

ACHIEVE TOP GRADES
A MUST FOR ALL STUDENTS

EVELYN SAMUEL on Priestley

Priestley's An Inspector Calls
Made Super Super Easy
First Edition Published by Evelyn Samuel
Copyright © 2020 Evelyn Samuel

EveMadeSuperEasyBooks
www.EveSuperEasyBooks.com
evesupereasybooks@gmail.com

DEDICATED TO

*My late brother Thiru Govender
who will forever be in my heart*

REVIEWS

★★★★★ **Excellent book**
Reviewed 17 January 2021
Very clear and well written book. Gives an excellent analysis of themes and characters.
Invaluable for study and gaining a clearer understanding of the text. Very highly recommended.
This has been highly helpful to my son with his GCSE studies. Would rate higher if I could!

★★★★★ **Informative**
Reviewed 20 February 2022
This book has helped me achieve grade 9 in my English lit gcse mocks. This book provides the best information about An Inspector Calls and will help you gain the grade you want.

★★★★★ **If you want to get a better level get this book**
Reviewed 8 October 2020
This book is amazing. I brought it for my son and now I am seeing great improvements in his work.
My son is now addicted to this, and it has helped him so much. My son went from a level 6 to a level 9 student. I thank the author of this book; thank you for making our lives easier for us.

★★★★★ **Fantastic resource!**
Reviewed 25 August 2021
Easy to follow guide. The kids absolutely love it! Definitely recommending to my friends and family.

★★★★★ **Excellent**
Reviewed 4 November 2020
This book is extremely helpful and covers all the information you need to help you secure the best grades in your GCSE exam. It has helped me improve my grades drastically.

★★★★★ **buy the book**
Reviewed 17 April 2021
This book goes into detail and gives you essay questions to help me improve with this book.
I recommend this book because it helped me change my grades to a level 8

★★★★★ **Very helpful**
Reviewed 6 November 2021
Very helpful guide that contains a ton of information.

★★★★★ **Very good**
Reviewed 25 October 2021
Excellent explanation easy to understand

★★★★★ **Want a Grade 9 in English literature?**
Reviewed 6 October 2020
I purchased this for my son in Y11, and he had told me that the book goes into a significant amount of depth and helped him boost his grade up by 2 grades. The level of explanation, detail and alterative viewpoints on how you can interpret different quotes, settings, characters etc. I definitely recommend this book for all GCSE students. My son said that it is better than all other revision guides.

★★★★★ **Want a Grade 9 in English literature?**
Reviewed 24 July 2021
Good book with full description and explanation with a great guide that helps with exam questions and you should get it.

PREFACE

To all students reading my study guide **An Inspector Calls made super super easy**. I do hope that my wealth of information will assist you to achieve the highest possible grades. I have formulated a unique structure where detailed explanations are next to the text to make it super super easy for you to connect and understand the book, and to revise without the need to resort to more than one book.

Each ACT is defined by a Summary followed by in-depth explanations which is highlighted with relevant important quotes. It identifies connotated meaning, imagery, symbolism, and linguistic devices. The context identifies the rationale behind the play, so that although Priestley wrote the play as a moralistic philosophical fictional detective story, the play essentially revolves around the social attitudes prevalent in society and directed towards the lower working class and the disposed prior to the First World War.

A detailed explanation of each main character in the book is provided so that the fabric of their relationships can be better understood. The social themes authenticate the human interactions portrayed in the book - the gulf between rich and poor. Typical exam questions are included to give some idea of the scope sought by the Exam Boards. Further details can be found in the Specification published by the Exam Boards on their websites. Answers to questions can be easily found in my text.

Finally, sample essays are provided to give you some idea of the standard expected by the Exam Boards.

Good Luck with your studies and your exam results.

FOREWARD

What a super super easy way to study and understand Priestley's 'An Inspector Calls'. No need to match text with explanation when both are next to each other.

I really enjoyed looking left at the text and right at the explanation. The structure and content of this fantastic book is a solid base to get to grip with this philosophical moralistic emotional fictional detective story where Inspector Goole subtly skilfully manipulates the suspects by his guile into revealing their guilt – the attitude engrained within society by the upper class at the time, where lower class workers like Eva Smith are disadvantaged and ultimately used and abused when they refuse to accept their status in society.

I can definitely recommend this study guide to all students, and hope they gain as much insight, as I did, into Priestley's 'An Inspector Calls'.

Teacher of English

**BOOKS PUBLISHED IN THE SERIES
MADE SUPER SUPER EASY**

Shakespeare's
MACBETH
ROMEO AND JULIET
OTHELLO
HAMLET

Priestley's
AN INSPECTOR CALLS

Dickens'
A CHRISTMAS CAROL

**SOON TO FOLLOW IN THE SERIES
MADE SUPER SUPER EASY**

Shakespeare's
THE TEMPEST
MID SUMMER NIGHT DREAM
MUCH ADO ABOUT NOTHING

**www.EveSuperEasyBooks.com
EveSuperEasyBooks@gmail.com**

CONTENTS

INTRODUCTION   **11**

PRIESTLEY   - Author   11
PLAY   - An Inspector Calls   11
CONTEXT   - George V's Britian   11

THE PLAY   **12**

CHARACTERS   12
SYNOPSIS   12
SETTING   13
FORM   14
STRUCTURE   14
LANGUAGE   15
PRODUCTION   16

TEXT AND EXPLANATIONS   **17**

ACT 1   **18**
  Summary   18
  Part 1   - Engagement Dinner   20
  Part 2   - Arthur and Gerald and Eric in conversion   28
  Part 3   - Inspector questions Arthur   33
  Part 4   - Inspector questions Sheila   39
  Part 5   - Inspector questions Gerald   46
ACT 2   **51**
  Summary   51
  Part 6   - Inspector questions both Sheila and Gerald   54
  Part 7   - Inspector questions both Sybil and Sheila   57
  Part 8   - Inspector questions Arthur again   61
  Part 9   - Inspector questions Sybil again   69
ACT 3   **79**
  Summary   79
  Part 10   - Inspector questions Eric   81
  Part 11   - Birlings in conversion   89
  Part 12   - Gerald telephones police to check-out Inspector   94
  Part 13   - Gerald debates Hoax with Birlings   96
  Part 14   - Gerald debates Photograph with Birlings   100
ENTRANCES AND EXITS   **106**

CHARACTERS   107

INSPECTOR GOOLE   107
ARTHUR BIRLING   110
SYBIL BIRLING   115
SHEILA BIRLING   118
ERIC BIRLING   121
GERALD CROFT   124
EVA SMITH alias Daisy Renton – later as Mrs Birling, Eric's wife   127

THEMES   130

SOCIAL RESPONSIBILTY   130
GENERATION GAP   132
POWER AND CLASS   135

SAMPLE ESSAYS   136

How Does Priestley Present the Inspector?   136
How is the Theme of Blame Explored?   139
How Does Priestley Explore and Develop the Birling Family?   142

TYPICAL Exam Style Questions   146

AUTHOR   152

PRIESTLEY

- J. B. Priestley wrote An Inspector Calls after the Second World War. In it, he tries to convey his controversial, politically charged message of social responsibility through the characters. His main aim was to pioneer a new morality in politics, due to his discontent with the rising social inequality in Britain.

THE PLAY

- The main underlying theme of the play is one of responsibility – "We are members of one body, we are responsible for each other."
- An Inspector Calls is a controversial play that was intended to convey Priestley's left-wing political ideology. He was a socialist, and he saw the capitalists as avaricious economic cannibals who lacked social responsibility. Because of this view, he wanted a better life for the proletariat workers like Eva Smith.
- The play was set in 1912 but was written in 1946. He uses dramatic irony to show the audience the vast differences between these eras and to clearly outline the dangers of capitalism. He vied for social mobility, embedding his views on socialism by building a strong socially responsible society.

CONTEXT

- In 1912, there were distinct differences between the rich, capitalist classes and the poor, socialist classes. In 1945, people were recovering from the war, and the class distinctions were markedly reduced.
- In 1912, women were subservient to men, and they had no rights. Women from the upper-class households got married to men from their own social class, whereas the women from poor, social backgrounds were seen as cheap labour. Eva Smith reflected this in the play. However, the role of women changed in 1946. They had to work and rebuild society, because the two world wars caused drastic fragmentation within the society.
- In 1912, the capitalist class did not change the status quo like the Birlings of the play. In 1946, however, there was a great move for social change.

CHARACTERS

INSPECTOR GOOLE	The man claiming to be a Police Inspector
ARTHUR BIRLING	The Business Man
SYBIL BIRLING	His Wife
SHEILA BIRLING	His Daughter
GERALD CROFT	Sheila's Fiancé
ERIC BIRLING	His Son
EDNA	The Maid
EVA SMITH	The worker sacked by Arthur for inciting worker's rights
alias **Daisy Renton**	sacked from next work place due to Sheila's jealousy
..alias **Mrs Birling** (Eric's wife)	denied support as a single parent by Sybil
	used and rejected as a mistress by both Gerald and Eric
	[does **NOT** appear in Play, just talked about]

SYNOPSIS

The mysterious **INSPECTOR GOOLE** arrives unannounced at the Birling's household while the family is celebrating the engagement of **SHEILA BIRLING** and **GERALD CROFT**. The **INSPECTOR** subtly but with firmness interrogates each member of the family about **EVA SMITH**, alias **DIASY RENTON**, who according to the **INSPECTOR** had committed suicide by swallowing disinfectant a few hours earlier.

By making use of **EVA'S** diary and her photo, the **INSPECTOR** is able to expose the guilt and remorse of those present. The **INSPECTOR** discovers that **EVA** was dismissed by **ARTHUR BIRLING** for inciting worker's rights; denied financial aid by **SYBIL BIRLING** because she aspired to elevate beyond her social class; made pregnant by **ERIC BIRLING** when drunk; falsely accused by **SHEILA BIRLING** contributing to her dismissal; and abandoned as a mistress by **GERALD CROFT**, the wealthy playboy.

Consequently, arguments ensue, with recriminations dividing into socialist and capitalist themes: **ERIC** and **SHEILA** empathising with **EVA'S** treatment and demise; **ARTHUR**, **SYBIL** and **GERALD** rejecting any wrongdoing. However, the **INSPECTOR** reminds everybody at the dinner party that all people are intertwined in one society. As he departs, he warns that, *"If men will not learn that lesson, then they will be taught in fire and blood and anguish"*, an allusion to tumult in society.

The mystery deepens when **ARTHUR** phones the police station only to discover that there is no **INSPECTOR GOOLE** on their staff. **GERALD** phones the Infirmary to discover that no girl had died by suicide that day. Relief turns to despondency when the phone suddenly rings; it is the police informing **ARTHUR BIRLING** that a police inspector is on the way to question everyone about the death of a girl who had just committed suicide by swallowing disinfectant.

In the play, Priestley is educating the reader on how the rich, capitalist class was out of touch with the sufferings of the poor socialist class.

SETTING

The play takes in the Birlings' **dining room** one evening in spring, 1912, the same year as the Titanic sailed on its ill-fated maiden voyage across the Atlantic Ocean. Priestley is meticulous as to the layout required to make the setting as realistic as possible: lighting, period furniture, period costumes, period etiquette and social standing. By not changing the set in each Act, Priestley creates a claustrophobic atmosphere, almost like being locked up in a police's interview room. The focus is always on the characters not the set.

In the Play, other locations talked about by the characters, which are essential to creating the intense and unremitting line of questioning pursued by the Inspector, are:

- **Brumley factory** owned by Arthur, where Eva Smith worked, and was then dismissed
- **Milwards' clothing shop**, where Eva Smith worked, and was then dismissed
- **The Palace Variety Theatre bar**, where Eva Smith met Alderman Meggarty, and was then rescued by Gerald to become his mistress, only to be rejected by him a few months later in September. In November, a drunken Eric picked up Eva Smith who became his mistress, but she left when she found out that Eric was giving her money stolen from the Arthur's factory.
- **The Brumley Women's Charity Organisation**, where Eva Smith was refused aid for her plight by Sybil, a prominent member.
- **The Hospital-Mortuary**, where according to Inspector Goole, Eva Smith died, but when Gerald phones the infirmary, is told there are no suicides, so consequently, Birling's and Gerald are sure it is a hoax perpetrated on them by the Inspector.
- **The Police Station**, where incoming calls were received by Arthur, and made by Gerald to establish the credentials of the Inspector and confirm any cases of suicides. A final call to Arthur, confirms that a girl had committed suicide, and an inspector was on the way to interview the Birlings.

An Inspector Calls is written in a dramatic style with moral overtones, but in a traditional form first used in France in the mid-19th century by Eugene Scribe. The plays are written in three acts in a naturalistic, realistic, or true to life, and usually features:

- **An Exposition** that informs the audience about characters, setting, context, themes and maybe intrigues to be revealed at some point later in the play.
- **Exits and Entrances** that are carefully timed to increase suspense and tension such as the Inspector's arrival in Act 1, where in a business like and serious manner starts his interrogation each character one at a time.
- **Past Actions** that precede the play such as the life and death of Eva Smith as revealed by Inspector Goole.
- **Revelations** that increase suspense and tension such as the use by the Inspector of Eva Smith's photo, shown individually to each character to unsettle them.
- **Cliff-hangers** at the end of Acts to increase suspense and tension such as Gerald's revelation to Sheila at the end of Act 1 that he did have an affair with Eva Smith.
- **One Plot** with no subplots such as the life and death of Eva Smith.
- **Obligatory Scene** where the main character Inspector Goole confronts the Birling's and guest Gerald Croft and succeeds in getting each of them to admit their part in the demise of Eva Smith.
- **The Denouement** that brings together all the elements necessary to make sense of the drama, but often a further surprise awaits, as Birling's and Gerald moods swing between elation that the event was a hoax, and fear of social disgrace when the play ends with the phone call from the police informing Arthur that a girl had just died on the way to the infirmary after swallowing some disinfectant, and a police inspector is on his way to ask some questions.

The characters are filtered into those such Arthur and Sybil who are detached from moral responsibility to those of the lower class in society; those such Sheila and Eric who feel remorse; and those such as Gerald who exhibit an indifference to Eva Smith's demise.

STRUCTURE

An Inspector Calls conforms to the Aristotle tradition that plays are structured according to the 'Three Unities':

- **unity of action** - one main plot that moves rapidly and smoothly (Eva Smith's demise)
- **unity of time** - the action takes place over a short period in real time (during dinner)
- **unity of place** - the action takes place in a single location (the dining room).

The characters are questioned individually in a particular order, so the plot is revealed.

Priestley uses realistic language appropriate to each character. The Inspector uses direct, uncompromising language. His direct style irritates Arthur and Sybil who find it offensive, confrontational, and disrespectful whereas Sheila, Eric, and Gerald find it intimidating and intrusive.

There are on occasions, odd words, and expressions peculiar to the era. Sheila remarks to Eric that he is "squiffy". In other words, a euphemism for inebriated or drunk.

LANGUAGE DEVICE: Speech

The dialogue defines the type of character and their personality. Arthur is a self-made business man aspiring to become a member of the wealthy upper class but retains his nonsense blunt self-opinionated rugged provincial speech. In contrast, his wife Sybil, son Eric, and daughter Sheila, are more refined in their speech being better educated. Gerald belongs to the upper class, so exhibits a more refined form of speech. His parents are Sir George Croft and Lady Croft. The Inspector uses assertive policemen speak.

LANGUAGE DEVICE: Rhetoric

Priestly uses rhetoric to persuade and convince others. Inspector Goole is determined to persuade the Birlings and Gerald of their guilt,

"This girl killed herself. But each of you helped to kill her. Remember that. Never forget it"

LANGUAGE DEVICE: Euphemism

The Inspector does not use euphemisms, so there is no vagueness to soften his stark questioning or statements. In contrast, Eric uses vague terms when referring to sexual matters, "And that's when it happened". Gerald uses the euphemism "keeping a girl" instead of the use of a 'working class call girl', so as to hide, the embarrassment of keeping a girl of lower social status than himself.

LANGUAGE DEVICE: Imagery

Priestley uses natural speech as spoken by the Edwardians in 19121, so there are few metaphors or similes in the play. However, in the Inspector's final speech to the Birlings and Gerald, emphasising the consequences of not taking moral responsibility, he says.

"fire and blood and anguish"

LANGUAGE DEVICE: Irony

Priestley uses irony to expose the double standards practised by the Birling and Gerald in the form of guilt. Secrets or lies. Gerald's deceit in not revealing his affair with Eva Smith alias Daisy Renton, or the dramatic irony when Sybil denies Eva support for her unborn child, not realising that Eric is the father, and had it been born, her grandchild.

The underling irony is that the Birlings and Gerald cannot envision that their way of life and duplicities will change. Within two years, the First World War caused a dramatic change in society, and by 1945, after the Second World War, when the play was first published, class divisions less prevalent.

LANGUAGE DEVICE: Irony

Priestley symbolism is wealth. Eva Smith is made penniless because wealthy people like Arthur and jealous people like Sheila have denied her work. Her only recourse to ask the Brumley Women's Charity Organisation for financial support, which was denied by Sybil, a prominent member of the board. Both Gerald and Eric showed no moral obligation. Gerald abandoned Eva because of class difference, and Eva abandoned Eric because he stole money from Arthur's factory to keep them.

PRODUCTION

The play was first produced in London on 1st October 1946 at the New Theatre.
All three acts, which are continuous, take place in the dining-room of the Birling's house in Brumley, an industrial city in the North Midlands.

It is an evening in spring, 1912.

The dining room of a fairly large suburban house, belonging to a prosperous manufacturer. It has good solid furniture of the period. The general effect is substantial and heavily comfortable, but not cosy and homelike. (If a realistic set is used, then it should be swung back, as it was in the production at the New Theatre. By doing this, you can have the dining-table centre downstage during Act One, when it is needed there, and then, swinging back, can reveal the fireplace for Act Two, and then for Act Three can show a small table with a telephone on it, downstage of fireplace. By this time the dining-table and its chairs have moved well upstage. Producers who wish to avoid this tricky business, which involves two re-settings of the scene and some very accurate adjustments of the extra flats necessary would be well advised to dispense of an ordinary realistic set, if only because the dining table becomes a nuisance. The lighting should be pink and intimate until the Inspector arrives, and then it should be brighter and harder.)

The text is written in the left column, and the explanation and interpretation, in the right column.

Important quotes and phrases in the text are highlighted and reproduced in the explanation column for discussion, on the same page. Consequently, there is no need to turn pages!

A summary of each Act precedes the text and explanation to give an overall perspective of the events in the story.

[BIRLING FAMILY – DINING ROOM]

The opening scene sets the tone and the pace of the play. All the action takes place in the house of a wealthy businessman, Mr Arthur Birling. It's a typical setting of the affluent Capitalist class at the time. Priestley does not leave out any details, 'large suburban house', 'prosperous manufacturer', 'port wine', 'cigar boxes', 'tails and ties', clearly reflecting the indulgence of the rich during the Edwardian era. It's a party setting with soft lighting and the atmosphere is happy and celebratory because Sheila is getting engaged to Gerald Croft. Priestley introduces the characters, and there is an air of cordiality among them. Sheila and Eric carry on some light-hearted banter.

"You are squiffy"

and this light-hearted banter changes into a more serious tone later in the play. We are properly introduced to a very imposing, pompous Mr Arthur Birling shown in the repetition of 'Hard-headed businessman'. His persistence that the Titanic won't sink. Once again, using repetition – 'Unsinkable, absolutely unsinkable'. His determination to show-off his superior knowledge, unfortunately, proves to be wrong. His need to be socially recognised is quite evident here when he talks about being 'Lord Mayor', and his chance of a 'Knighthood'. Ironically, just before the Inspector's arrival he relays his pivotal speech to Gerald and Eric about social responsibility.

"A man has to make his own way and look after himself and his family too."

The main theme that Priestley emphasises in the play is one of responsibility. Clearly, we can detect from Mr Birling's speech that he has no concern for social responsibility because his speech here reeks of selfishness. Ironically, Priestley's timing is perfect because the Inspector enters at this opportune time.

[THE ARRIVAL OF THE INSPECTOR]

Edna, the maid announces the Inspector's arrival. Mr Arthur Birling is in high spirits,

"And feeling contented, for once"

continuing,

"I am still on the bench. It may be something about a warrant."

Ironically, his confidence wanes once the Inspector arrives and questions him. The Inspector is described as a man of massiveness, solidity, and purposefulness.

Mr Arthur Birling is immediately trying to impress the Inspector,

"I was an Alderman for years – and Lord Mayor."

We can once again, note Mr Arthur Birling's need to be socially recognised. When questioned by the Inspector, Mr Birling cannot recall who Eva Smith was after the Inspector's revelation,
> "I seem to remember hearing that name – Eva Smith – somewhere."

After seeing the photograph, Mr Birling admits to knowing her.
> "She was a lively good – looking girl."

He also admits that he had refused her demand for higher rates, and fired her.
> "She'd had a lot to say – far too much – so she had to go."

[THE INSPECTOR QUESTIONING SHEILA]

We see a very cheerful Sheila who gaily skips into the room and is quite puzzled about the situation that is unfolding before her because the Inspector refused for them to leave the room.
> "What's all this about?"

she enquires. She also strikes us as being rather curious.
> "What business? What's happening?"

Her mood has instantly changed when she hears about Eva Smith's death. Her reaction was instantaneous, one of sympathy and shock. Note Sheila's and Eric's reaction to the news as juxtaposed to Mr Birling's. Mr Birling was cold and detached whereas Sheila and Eric empathised with Eva Smith's situation. We can deduce that Sheila and Eric were Priestley's vision for the future because they took responsibility whereas Mr Birling – from the older generation said,
> "Still I can't accept any responsibility."

During her conversation with the Inspector, Sheila is very naïve because she is very unaware at this point that she was involved in Eva Smith's death. When she sees the photograph, she, 'gives a half-stifled sob, and then runs out'. Clearly, she is visibly shaken and remorseful, and she goes on to say,
> "So I am really responsible."

[INSPECTOR GOOLE REMAINS AT THE DOOR]

START OF PART 1

MR ARTHUR BIRLING

MRS SYBIL BIRLING

SHEILA BIRLING

ERIC BIRLING

GERALD CROFT

[BIRLINGS AND GERALD AT DINNER]

Priestley gives us a vivid description of the Birling's house.

'A fairly large suburban house,' typical of the Capitalist class which Mr Birling represent. It had 'solid furniture' like their solid lives, but that solidity will soon be broken when the Inspector arrives.

Priestley says that the general effect is heavily comfortable. Mr Birling is described as 'heavy-looking'. The house was also described as, 'not cosy and homelike' and Mrs Birling is described as, 'a rather cold woman'.

One can associate their personalities to their furniture which are inanimate objects – cold and detached. The lighting is 'pink and intimate', in keeping with the celebratory nature of Sheila's engagement but we see a tone change when the Inspector arrives.

// The dining room is of a fairly large suburban house, belonging to a prosperous manufacturer. It has a good solid furniture of the period.

The general effect is a substantial and heavily comfortable but not cosy and homelike.

The lighting is pink and intimate until the Inspector arrives, and then changes to brighter and harder.

At rise of curtain, the four BIRLINGS and GERALD are seated at the table, with ARTHUR BIRLING at one end, his wife at the other, ERIC downstage and SHEILA and GERALD seated upstage.
EDNA, the parlour maid, is just clearing the table, which has no cloth, of the dessert plates and champagne glasses, etc, and then replacing them with decanter of port, cigar box and cigarettes. Port glasses are already on the table. All five are in evening dress of the period, the men in tails and white ties, not dinner-jackets. ARTHUR BIRLING is a heavy-looking, rather portentous man in his middle fifties with fairly easy manners but rather provincial in this speech. His wife is about fifty, a rather cold woman and her husband's social superior. SHEILA is a pretty girl in her early twenties, very pleased with life and rather excited. GERALD CROFT is an attractive chap about thirty, rather too manly to be a dandy but very much the well-bred young man-about-town. ERIC is in his early twenties, not quite at ease, half shy, half assertive. At the moment they have all had a good dinner, are celebrating a special occasion, and are pleased with themselves. //

Arthur Birling: Giving us the port, Edna? That's right. (*he pushes it towards Eric..*) You ought to like this port, Gerald, as a matter of fact, Finchley told me it's exactly the same port your father gets from him.

Gerald: Then it'll be all right. The governor prides himself on being a good judge of port. I don't pretend to know much about it.

The lighting gets brighter and harder which can be associated with the terrible news that the Inspector is bringing. We see the indulgence of the rich, Capitalist class with fancy attire –
'tails, and white bow ties, evening dresses and stylish tables set with port, cigar box and cigarettes.'

Priestley deliberately details their decadent lifestyle to show us how the poor Socialist class like Eva Smith were struggling without food or jobs, yet the rich of that era lived in such opulence.

His description of Mr and Mrs Birling is not very flattering, and one can connote that he writes with a bitter tone – Mr Birling a rather portentous man; his wife, a rather cold woman. Sheila is very pleased with life. We see a gradual change in Sheila from a naïve, impressionable young girl to one who is strong and mature by the end of the play. Gerald is described as the,
'easy, well-bred young man-about-town.'
Eric, 'not quite at ease, half-shy, half-assertive'.

They are celebrating the very special occasion – Sheila's engagement. They are very pleased with themselves, but this excitement is short-lived with the arrival of the Inspector.

The BIRLINGS and GERALD CROFT at Dinner

Mr Birling is very patronising when he talks about port. He is trying to emulate Mr Croft by copying his taste in wine.

"It's exactly the same port your father gets"

Sheila: (*gaily, possessively*) I should jolly well think not, Gerald, I'd hate you to know all about port – like one of these purple-faced old men.

Arthur Birling: Here, I'm not a purple-faced old man.
Sheila Birling: no, not yet. But then you don't know all about port – do you?
Birling: (*noticing that his wife has not taken any*) Now then, Sybil, you must a take a little tonight. Special occasion, y'know, eh?
Sheila: Yes, go on, mummy. You must drink our health.
Mrs Birling: (*smiling*) Very well, then. Just a little, thank you. (*to Edna, who is about to go, with tray.*) all right, Edna. I'll ring from the drawing room when we want coffee. Probably in about half an hour.
Edna: (*going*) Yes, ma'am.

// *Edna goes out. They now have all the glasses filled. Birling beams at them and clearly relaxes.*//

Birling: Well, well – this is very nice. Very nice. Good dinner too, Sybil. Tell cook from me.
Gerald: (*politely*) Absolutely first class.

Mrs Birling: (*reproachfully*) Arthur, you're not supposed to say such things-

Birling: Oh – come, come – I'm treating Gerald like one of the family. And I'm sure he won't object.
Sheila: (*with mocking aggressiveness*) Go on, Gerald – just you object!
Gerald: (*smiling*) Wouldn't dream of it. In fact, I insist upon being one of the family now. I've been trying long enough, haven't I? (*as she does not reply, with more insistence.*) Haven't I? You know I have.
Mrs Birling: (*smiling*) Of course she does.

Sheila: (*half serious, half playful*) Yes – except for all last summer, when you never came near me, and I wondered what had happened to you.

Gerald: And I've told you – I was awfully busy at the works all that time.

He is trying to equate his status to that of the Crofts who are far superior. In the stage direction we note that Sheila is described as 'gaily'. We will trace her mood changes throughout the play.

"I'd hate you to know all about port"

Later we see that her reaction to Gerald's infidelity is far more serious.
When Mr Birling compliments the cook, Mrs Birling reproached him for saying so,

"Arthur, you are not supposed to say such things-"

Mrs Birling proves to be a social snob, a typical behaviour of aristocratic women of that era.

Sheila is very perceptive when she questions Gerald about his absence all summer,

"When you never came near me"

This can be foreshadowing for later in the play when Gerald's affair is revealed.

SHEILA BIRLING with fiancé **GERALD CROFT**

TEXT ACT 1 part 1	EXPLANATION
Sheila: (*same tone as before*) Yes, that's what you say.	Sheila is suspicious of him, and her suspicions are later confirmed.
Mrs Birling: Now, Sheila, don't tease him. When you're married you'll realize that men with important work to do sometimes have to spend nearly all their time and energy on their business. You'll have to get used to that, just as I had.	"Yes, that's what you say"
Sheila: I don't believe I will. (*half playful, half serious, to Gerald.*) So you be careful.	Sheila tends to be assertive here when she tells Gerald, "So you be careful"
Gerald: Oh – I will, I will.	It's more like a threat and we can see that Sheila is already developing and is standing up for her rights. Sheila and Eric share a light banter which is typical of the younger generation,
//Eric suddenly guffaws. His parents look at him.//	"You're squiffy",
Sheila: (*severely*) Now – what's the joke? Eric: I don't know – really. Suddenly I felt I just had to laugh.	"Don't be an ass, Eric"
Sheila: You're squiffy.	Sheila's use of colloquialism shocks snobbish Mrs Birling.
Eric: I'm not.	"What an expression Sheila!"
Mrs Birling: What an expression, Sheila! Really the things you girls pick up these days!	Mr Birling is excited about the union between Sheila and Gerald, and this could mean a merger between the Croft's and the Birling's companies. We can also connote that this union is more like a business contract because in Edwardian times marrying into rich families meant a secured social status.
Eric: If you think that's the best she can do-	
Sheila: Don't be an ass, Eric.	
Mrs Birling: Now stop it, you two. Arthur, what about this famous toast of yours? Birling: Yes, of course. (*clears his throat.*) Well, Gerald, I know you agreed that we should only have this quiet little family party. It's a pity sir George and – we – Lady Croft can't be with us, but they're abroad and so it can't be helped. As I told you, they sent me a very nice cable – couldn't be nicer. I'm not sorry that we're celebrating quietly like this-	
Mrs Birling: Much nicer really.	
Gerald: I agree.	
Birling: So do I, but it makes speech-making more difficult-	
Eric: (*not too rudely*) Well, don't do any. We'll drink their health and have done with it.	

ERIC BIRLING

Birling: No, we won't. It's one of the happiest nights of my life. And one day, I hope, Eric, when you've a daughter of your own, you'll understand why. Gerald, I'm going to tell you frankly, without any pretences, that your engagement to Sheila means a tremendous lot to me. She'll make you happy, and I'm sure you'll make her happy. You're just the kind of son-in-law I always wanted. Your father and I have been friendly rivals in business for some time now – though Crofts limited are both older and bigger than Birling and company – and now you've brought us together, and perhaps we may look forward to the time when Crofts and Birlings are no longer competing but are working together – for lower costs and higher prices.

Gerald: Hear, hear! And I think my father would agree to that.
Mrs Birling: Now, Arthur, I don't think you ought to talk business on an occasion like this.
Sheila: Neither do I. All wrong.
Birling: Quite so, I agree with you. I only mentioned it in passing. What I did want to say was – that Sheila's a lucky girl – and I think you're a pretty fortunate young man too, Gerald.
Gerald: I know I am – this once anyhow.
Birling: (raising his glass) So here's wishing the pair of you – the very best that life can bring. Gerald and Sheila.
Mrs Birling: (raising her glass, smiling) Yes, Gerald. Yes, Sheila darling. Our congratulations and very best wishes!
Gerald: Thank you.
Mrs Birling: Eric!
Eric: (rather noisily) All the best! She's got a nasty temper sometimes – but she's not bad really. Good old Sheila!

Sheila: Chump! I can't drink to this, can I? When do I drink?

Mr Birling says,

"It's one of the happiest nights of my life"

Because of this union and the merger of their companies, they can work together

"for lower costs and higher prices"

Priestley clearly shows us how the capitalist class get rich at the expense of the poor, Socialist class.

Mrs Birling rebukes Arthur Birling for talking too much business and not celebrating the occasion of Sheila and Gerald's engagement.

"Now, Arthur, I don't think you ought to talk business on an occasion like this"

Instead, Mrs Birling raises her glass to Sheila and Gerald,

"Our congratulations and very best wishes!"

MRS SYBIL BIRLING

Sheila is slightly embarrassed when Eric makes a snide comment about her,

"She's got a nasty temper sometimes – but she's not bad really"

Gerald: You can drink to me.
Sheila: (*quiet and serious now*) All right then. I drink to you, Gerald.

//for a moment they look at each other//

Gerald: (*quietly*) Thank you. And I drink to you – and hope I can make you as happy as you deserve to be.
Shelia: (*trying to be light and easy*) You be careful – or I'll start weeping.
Gerald: (*smiling*) Well, perhaps this will help to stop it. (*he produces a ring case.*)

Sheila: (*excited*) Oh – Gerald – you've got it – is it the one you wanted me to have?

Gerald: (*giving the case to her*) Yes – the very one.
Sheila: (*taking out the ring*) Oh – it's wonderful! Look – mummy – isn't it a beauty? Oh – darling -
(*she kisses Gerald hastily.*)
Eric: Steady the buffs!
Sheila: (*who has put the ring on, admiringly*) I think it's perfect. Now I really feel engaged.
Mrs Birling: So you ought, darling. It's a lovely ring. Be careful with it.

Sheila: Careful! I'll never let it go out of my sight for an instant.

Mrs Birling: (*smiling*) Well, it came just at the right moment. That was clever of you, Gerald. Now, Arthur, if you've no more to say, I think Sheila and I had better go into the drawing room and leave you men-

Birling: (*rather heavily*) I just want to say this. (*noticing that Sheila is still admiring her ring.*) Are you listening, Sheila? This concerns you too. And after all I don't often make speeches at you-

Sheila: I'm sorry, daddy. Actually I was listening.

//she looks attentive, as they all do. He holds them for a moment before continuing. //

Gerald relieves the situation by saying,

"You can drink to me"

Sheila, quiet and serious now, replies

All right then, I drink to you, Gerald

SHEILA put on Engagement Ring

Gerald gives Sheila a ring and she is rather excited,

"Is it the one you wanted me to have?"

During Edwardian times men were the dominant figure and women were subservient to them. We can see here that Sheila had no say in choosing the ring. She says that she will never,

"let it go out of my sight for an instant"

Ironically, later in the play she throws it back at Gerald when she learns of his affair with Eva Smith. Mr Birling is about to make a speech and he notices that Sheila is still admiring the ring. He treats her like a child and asks,

"Are you listening Sheila?"

To which she promptly responds,

"I am sorry Daddy. Actually, I was listening."

As the play progresses, we see Sheila's development from this subservient girl to a strong, powerful woman at the end of the play

<u>Birling</u>: I'm delighted about this engagement and I hope it won't be too long before you're married. And I want to say this. There's a good deal of silly talk about these days – but – and I speak as a hard-headed business man, who has to take risks and know what he's about – I say, you can ignore all this silly pessimistic talk. When you marry, you'll be marrying at a very good time. Yes, a very good time – and soon it'll be an even better time. Last month, just because the miners came out on strike, there's a lot of wild talk about possible labour trouble in the near future. Don't worry. We've passed the worst of it. We employers at last are coming together to see that our interests – and the interests of capital – are properly protected. And we're in for a time of steadily increasing prosperity.

   <u>Gerald</u>: I believe you're right, sir.
   <u>Eric</u>: What about war?

   <u>Birling</u>: Glad you mentioned it, Eric. I'm coming to that. Just because the Kaiser makes a speech or two, or a few German officers have too much to drink and begin taking nonsense, you'll hear some people say that war's inevitable. And to that I say – fiddlesticks! The Germans don't want war. Nobody wants war, except some half-civilized folks in the Balkans. And why? There's too much at stake these days. Everything to lose and nothing to gain by war.

   <u>Eric</u>: Yes, I know – but still –

   <u>Birling</u>: Just let me finish, Eric. You've a lot to learn yet. And I'm taking as a hard headed, practical man of business. And I say there isn't a chance of war. The world's developing so fast that it'll make war impossible. Look at the progress we're making. In a year or two we'll have aeroplanes that will be able to go anywhere. And look at the way the auto-mobile's making headway – bigger and faster all the time. And then ships. Why, a friend of mine went over this new liner last week – the titanic – she sails next week – forty-six thousand eight hundred tons – New York in five days – and every luxury – and unsinkable, absolutely unsinkable.

Mr Birling make repeated references to

"hard-headed business man,"

and he does it with a tone of pride.

He also very lightly dismisses the miner's strike and trouble with the Labour party who protect the interest of the proletariat (working class) and concentrates on making his profits.

"And we're in for a time of steadily increasing prosperity"

He also demeans the Balkans,

"half-civilised folks in the Balkans"

He also misjudges when he says that there will be no war, yet two years later war breaks-out.

We can draw an imagery about the 'Titanic'. Mr Birling's confidence is boosted when he again uses repetition when discussing the Titanic,

"and unsinkable, absolutely unsinkable"

We can associate Mr Birling as a symbol of the Titanic and believed that he was a strong pillar of society, and he could never sink or be brought down. But when the Inspector comes and interrogates him, he sunk just like the Titanic because the Inspector eventually had the upper hand over Mr Birling. One example of this is when the Inspector agreed for Eric to have a drink but then Mr Birling declined. Mr Birling had to later follow the Inspector's directive and he allowed Eric a drink.

Birling: (*continues*)	
That's what you've got to keep your eye on, facts like that, progress like that – and not a few German officers taking nonsense and a few scaremongers here making a fuss about nothing.	For the future, Mr Birling is confident that
Now you three young people, just listen to this – and remember what I'm telling you now. In twenty or thirty years' time – let's say, in 1940 – you may be giving a little party like this – your son or daughter might be getting engaged – and I tell you, by that time you'll be living in a world that'll have forgotten all these capital versus labour agitations and all these silly little war scares. There'll be peace and prosperity and rapid progress everywhere – except of course in Russia, which will always be behindhand naturally.	"There'll be peace and prosperity and rapid progress everywhere"

except in Russia where business and life are backward,

"Russia which will always be behindhand naturally." |
| Mrs Birling: Arthur! | Mrs Birling reminds her husband, not to keep Gerald too long because there are more important things to talk about other than business. |
| // has Mrs Birling shows signs of interrupting. // | |
| Birling: Yes, my dear, I know – I'm talking too much. But you youngsters just remember what I Said. We can't let these Bernard Shaw's and H.G.Wellses do all the talking. We hard-headed practical business men must say something sometime. And we don't guess – we've had experience - and we know. | Mr Birling acknowledges this fact,

"Yes, my dear, I know – I'm talking too much"

but retorts with,

"We hard-headed practical business men must say something sometime" |
Mrs Birling. (*rising. The others rise*) Yes, of course, dear. Well don't keep Gerald in here too long. Eric – I want you a minute.	
// she and Sheila *and* Eric *go out*. Birling *and* Gerald *sit down again.* //	
END OF PART 1	

START OF PART 2

Birling: Cigar?

Gerald: No, thanks. Can't really enjoy them.

Birling: (*taking one himself*) Ah, you don't know what you're missing. I like a good cigar. (*indicating decanter.*) Help yourself.

Gerald: Thank you.

// Birling *lights his cigar and Gerald, who had lit a cigarette, helps himself to port, then pushes the decanter to Birling.* //

Birling: Thanks. (*confidentially*) By the way, there's something I'd like to mention – in strict confidence – while we're by ourselves. I have an idea that your mother – Lady Croft – while she doesn't object to my girl – feels you might have done better for yourself socially -

// Gerald, *rather embarrassed, begins to murmur some dissent, but* Birling *checks him.* //

No, Gerald, that's all right. Don't blame her. She comes from an old country family – landed people and so forth – and so it's only natural. But what I wanted to say is – there's a fair chance that I might find my way into the next Honours list. Just a knighthood, of course.

Gerald: Oh – I say – congratulations!

Birling: Thanks, but it's a bit too early for that. So don't say anything. But I've had a hint or two. You see, I was Lord Mayor here two years ago when royalty visited us. And I've always been regarded as a sound useful party man. So – well – I gather there's a very good chance of a knighthood – so long as we behave ourselves, don't get into the police court or start a scandal – eh? (*laughs complacently.*)

Gerald: (*laughs*) You seem to be a nice well-behaved family -

Birling: We think we are -

Mr Birling, always conscious of his social status tells Gerald that his mother might think that he could have done better socially instead of him marrying Sheila

"feels you might have done better for yourself socially"

In order to show Gerald that he will be rising in social status, he tells Gerald of his chance of getting a Knighthood,

"Just a Knighthood, of course"

Mr Birling goes on blowing his own trumpet, trying to impress Gerald when he says,

"I was Lord Mayor here two years ago when royalty visited us"

Priestley's use of irony is very apt here when Mr Birling says,

"so long as we behave ourselves, don't get into the police court or start a scandal"

Well later the police Inspector comes with news of a scandal that the Birlings are involved in. Gerald laughs and says,

"you seem to be a nice well-behaved family"

The use of the article 'seem' tells us that the Birling's lifestyle is superficial and an example of this is their ugly treatment of Eva Smith.

Mr Birling's business-like reply is,

"We think we are"-

Gerald: So if that's the only obstacle, sir, I think you might as well accept my congratulations now.

Birling: No, no, I couldn't do that. And don't say anything yet.

Gerald: Not even to my mother? I know she'd be delighted.

Birling: Well, when she comes back, you might drop a hint to her. And you can promise her that we'll try to keep out of trouble during the next few months.

//*they both laugh.* Eric *enters*//

Eric: What's the joke? Started telling stories?

Birling: No. want another glass of port?

Eric: (*sitting down*) Yes, please. (*takes decanter and helps himself.*) Mother says we mustn't stay too long. But I don't think it matters. I left 'em talking about clothes again. You'd think a girl had never any clothes before she gets married. Women are potty about 'em.

Birling: Yes, but you've got to remember, my boy, that clothes mean something quite different to a woman. Not just something to wear – and not only something to make 'em look prettier – but – well, a sort of sign or token of their self-respect.

Gerald: That's true.
Eric: (*eagerly*) Yes, I remember – (*but he checks himself.*)
Birling: Well, what do you remember?
Eric: (*confused*) Nothing.
Birling: Nothing?
Gerald: (*amused*) Sounds a bit fishy to me.

Birling: (*taking it in the same manner*) Yes, you don't know what some of these boys get up to nowadays. More money to spend and time to spare than I had when I was Eric's age. They worked us hard in those days and kept us short of cash. Thought even then – we broke out and had a bit of fun sometimes.
Gerald: I'll bet you did.

Mr Birling is keen for Gerald's mother to know about his Knighthood so that he will be more socially accepted by her,

"You might drop a hint to her"

[ERIC ENTERS]

ERIC BIRLING

Mr Birling offers Eric a glass of wine. Priestley uses a clothing imagery here to highlight the Birling's superficial lifestyle. When Eric tells them that he left the women talking about clothes.

"Clothes mean something quite different to a woman"

"well, a sort of sign or token of their self-respect"

A sense of hypocrisy is highlighted here when we think about how Sheila got Eva Smith fired from the dress shop because of some trivial whim of hers. Simply because Eva Smith looked better than her in the dress. She surely didn't show any self-respect there.

In another one of his many speeches, Mr Birling ironically states,

"Yes, you don't know what some of these boys get up to nowadays."

Birling: (*solemnly*) But this is the point. I don't want to lecture you two young fellows again.

But what so many of you don't seem to understand now, when things are so much easier, is that a man has to make his own way – has to look after himself – and his family too, of course, when he has one – and so long as he does that he won't come to much harm.

But the way some of these cranks talk and write now,

you'd think everybody has to look after everybody else,

as if we were all mixed up together like bees in a hive –

community and all that nonsense.

But take my word for it, you youngsters – and I've learnt in the good hard school of experience

that a man has to mind his own business and look after himself and his own – and -

// we hear the sharp ring of a door bell. Birling stops to listen. //

Eric: Somebody at the front door.
Birling: Edna'll answer it. Well, have another glass of port, Gerald – and then we'll join the ladies. That'll stop me giving you good advice.
Eric: Yes, you've piled it on a bit tonight, Father.
Birling: Special occasion. And feeling contented, for once, I wanted you to have the benefit of my experience.

// Edna *enters*//

Edna: Please, sir, an Inspector's called.
Birling: An Inspector? What kind of Inspector?
Edna: A police Inspector. He says his name's Inspector Goole.
Birling: Don't know him. Does he want to see me
Edna: Yes, sir. He says it's important.

Mr Birling gives us an indication of how hard he worked to climb the social ladder. He wasn't born rich like his wife.

"They worked us hard in those days."

When Mr Birling lectures to Eric and Gerald, he tells them,

"that a man has to make his own way – has to look after himself - and his family too"

It's obvious here that he is instilling in the boy's a sense of selfishness and this speech is void of any social responsibility. Mr Birling bitterly voiced his opinion about his dislike of socialism.

"But the way some of these cranks talk and write now"

He doesn't want his family to be socially responsible for the poor, like Eva Smith.

"You'd think everybody has to look after everybody else"

He goes on to use an animal imagery,

"as if we were all mixed up together like bees in a hive-"

The simile here suggesting that Mr Birling is convinced that we are not animals living in a communal setting and helping each other, like bees who have specific duties to perform in a hive and everybody works and help each other,

"community and all that nonsense."

It's very important that we take careful note of Mr Birling's last speech here and it's timing.

"that a man has to mind, his own business and look after himself and his own – and "

Birling: All right, Edna. Show him in here. Give us some more light.

// Edna *does, then goes out.* //

I'm still on the Bench. It may be something about a warrant.

Gerald: (*lightly*) Sure to be. Unless Eric's been up to something. (*nodding confidentially to Birling.*) And that would be awkward, wouldn't it?

Birling: (*humorously*) Very.
Eric: (*who is uneasy, sharply*) Here, what do you mean?

The symbol of the bell is important here. Its sharp ring is symbolic, it's like a warning to the Birling's to start mending their ways. Ironically at the very end of the play we hear the telephone, 'rings sharply' and a 'real' police inspector is on his way to question them and show them the error of their ways.

When Edna announces the arrival of the Inspector, Mr Birling asks her to

"Give us some more light"

The use of light imagery here can suggest that Mr Birling needs to see the light and change his selfish attitude and his negative way of thinking. Mr Birling's pompous attitude surfaces once again when he assumes that the Inspector came to see him about a warrant.

"I am still on the bench. It may be something about a warrant"

Gerald's response is ironical because he hits out at Eric's behaviour. Gerald himself is not so innocent but is pretending to be the perfect gentleman and very ready to point fingers at Eric. His sense of hypocrisy is glowing here because he is just as guilty of the same atrocity that Eric is guilty of. He too, we later find out is guilty of having an affair with Eva Smith.

"Unless Eric's been up to something.
And that would be awkward, wouldn't it"

Well Eric has been up to something which will soon be revealed by the Inspector. Eric is always described as,

'not quite at ease,' 'uneasy' and still uneasy by the stage directions.

This tells us that Eric does not possess adequate self-confidence and we can also note that there is a certain cold detachment between him and his father.

Gerald: (*lightly*) Only something we were talking about when you were out. A joke really.

Eric: (*still uneasy*) Well, I don't think it's very funny.

Birling: (*sharply, staring at him*) What's the matter with you?

Eric: (*defiantly*) Nothing.

Edna: (*opening door, and announcing*) Inspector Goole.

INSPECTOR GOOLE

END OF PART 2

Actually, if we look carefully, we see that Gerald is more favoured and respected by Mr Birling than Eric. Note that Mr Birling offers Gerald a drink but he doesn't offer Eric one.

Gerald was very bold to actually tell Eric that he and Mr Birling discuss business affairs and he is the subject of other jokes.

"A joke really."

This will indicate that Mr Birling is more cordial to Gerald than to his own son. Eric is still uneasy and he says that he doesn't think it's funny.

"Well, I don't think it's very funny."

Ironically, if we judge Gerald's character, we see that he appears to be a pillar of society but in reality, he is not because he too was responsible for Eva Smith's demise. He was very callous in having an affair with her and deserting her.

The rich capitalist class in the Edwardian era had many skeletons in their cupboards. Here it's the case of the 'pot calling the kettle black', because Gerald is picking on Eric, yet he too had an affair with Eva Smith. There is a tense situation between Eric and Mr Birling because Mr Birling speaks sharply to him, stares at him and asks,

"What's the matter with you?"

Eric's response is one of defiance when he retorts,

"Nothing"

It's blatantly clear here that Mr Birling is annoyed with Eric for telling Gerald off,

Now we are made well aware of Eric's insecurity and uneasiness because of Mr Birling's emotional detachment from him.

START OF PART 3

INSPECTOR GOOLE

// the inspector *enters, and* Edna *goes, closing door after her. The* inspector *need not be a big man but he creates at once an impression of massiveness, solidity and purposefulness. He is a man in his fifties, dressed in a plain darkish suit of the period. He speaks carefully, weightily, and has a disconcerting habit of looking hard at the person he addresses before actually speaking. //*

Inspector: Mr Birling?
Birling: Yes. Sit down inspector.
Inspector: (*sitting*) Thank you, sir.
Birling: Have a glass of port – or a little whisky?
Inspector: No, thank you, Mr Birling. I'm on duty.
Birling: You're new, aren't you?
Inspector: Yes, sir. Only recently transferred.
Birling: I thought you must be. I was an alderman for years – and Lord Mayor two years ago – and I'm still on the Bench – so I know the Brumley police offices pretty well – and I thought I'd never seen you before.
Inspector: Quite so.
Birling: Well, what can I do for you? Some trouble about a warrant?
Inspector: No, Mr Birling.
Birling: (*after a pause, with a touch of impatience*) Well, what is it then?

[THE INSPECTOR ENTERS]

INSPECTOR introduced by EDNA the Maid

The Inspector acts as Priestley's voice because he is here to convey Priestley's message of Social Responsibility. He assumes a God-like status and he is an omniscient character. The Inspector creates an impression of:

'*massiveness, solidity and purposefulness*'

He is dressed in 'a plain darkish suit'.

This colour imagery can suggest that the darkish suit that the Inspector is wearing can be associated with the dark news that he brought.

ARTHUR – GERALD – GOOLE – ERIC

Almost immediately and before the Inspector has stated his business, Mr Birling brags about being 'Lord mayor' and 'on the bench' and that he knows the police officers well. Once again, putting his social status on display.

Inspector: I'd like some information, if you don't mind, Mr Birling. Two hours ago a young woman died on the infirmary. She'd been taken there this afternoon because she'd swallowed a lot of strong disinfectant. Burnt her inside out, of course.

Eric: (*involuntarily*) My god!

Inspector: Yes, she was in great agony. They did everything they could for her at the infirmary, but she died. Suicide, of course.

Birling: (*rather impatiently*) Yes, yes. Horrid business. But I don't understand why you should come here, Inspector –

Inspector: (*cutting through, massively*) I've been round to the room she had, and she'd left a letter there and a sort of diary. Like a lot of these young women who get into various kinds of trouble, she'd used more than one name. But her original name – her real name – was Eva Smith.

Birling: (*thoughtfully*) Eva Smith?

Inspector: Do you remember her, Mr Birling?

Birling: (*slowly*) No – I seem to remember hearing that name – Eva Smith – somewhere. But it doesn't convey anything to me. And I don't see where I come into this.

Inspector: She was employed in your works at one time.

Birling: Oh – that's it, is it? Well, we've several hundred young women there, y'know, and they keep changing.

Inspector: This young women, Eva Smith, was out of the ordinary. I found a photograph of her in her lodgings. Perhaps you'd remember her from that.

// *inspector takes a photograph, about postcard size, out of his pocket and goes to* Birling. *Both* Gerald *and* Eric *rise to have a look at the photograph, but the inspector interposes himself between them and the photograph. They are surprised and rather annoyed.* Birling *stares hard, and with recognition, at the photograph, which the* inspector *then replaces in his pocket.* //

The Inspector tells Mr Birling about his investigation of how a woman died in the Infirmary and she was,

"Burnt her inside out."

The Inspector's use of violent graphic imagery is very effective and is meant for Mr Birling to visualise the scenario and empathise, but his reaction is far from empathy whereas Eric's reaction is full of empathy,

"My God!"

The exclamation suggest his shock and we can juxtapose his reaction to that of Mr Birling's which was cold and detached.

"She was one of my employees and then I discharged her."

Priestley didn't like how the older generation behaved towards the poor socialist class and Eric is Priestley's vision for the future. He wants the younger generation to create social mobility in society and take responsibility. The stage directions tell us of Mr Birling's impatience 'Touch of impatience', 'rather impatiently', and his use of short, snappy sentences,

"yes, yes. Horrid business"

makes it clear to us that he doesn't care about Eva Smith's situation, and he just wants to get over with the questioning quickly. When the Inspector asks Mr Birling if he knew who Eva Smith was:

"I seem to remember hearing that name"

This proves how detached he was from his workers.

We take a close look at the Inspector's very clever techniques which creates a lot of suspense, hence firing up the reader's curiosity.

Gerald: (*showing annoyance*) Any particular reason why I shouldn't see this girl's photograph, Inspector?

Inspector: (*coolly, looking hard at him*) There might be.

Eric: And the same applies to me, I suppose?

Inspector: Yes

Gerald: I can't imagine what it could be.

Eric: Neither can I.

Birling: And I must say, I agree with them, Inspector.

Inspector: It's the way I like to go to work. One person and one line of inquiry at a time. Otherwise, there's a muddle.

Birling: I see. Sensible really. (*moves restlessly, then turns.*) you've had enough of that port, Eric.

// the Inspector is watching Birling *and now* Birling *notices him. //*

Inspector: I think you remember Eva Smith now don't you. Mr Birling?

Birling: Yes, I do. She was one of my employees and then I discharged her.

Eric: Is that why she committed suicide? When was this, father?

Birling: Just keep quiet, Eric, and don't get excited. This girl left us nearly two years ago. Let me see – it must have been in the early autumn of nineteen-ten.

Inspector: Yes. End of September, nineteen-ten.

Birling: That's right.

Gerald: Look here, sir. Wouldn't you rather I was out of this?

Birling: I don't mind your being here, Gerald. And I'm sure you've no objection, have you, inspector? Perhaps I ought to explain first that this is Mr Gerald Croft – the son of sir George Croft – you know, Crofts limited.

Inspector: Mr Gerald Croft, eh?

Birling: Yes. Incidentally we've been modestly celebrating his engagement to my daughter, Sheila.

Inspector: I see. Mr Croft is going to marry Miss Sheila Birling?

MR BIRLING with EVA SMITH's photograph

He shows the photograph of Eva Smith only to Mr Birling. When Eric and Gerald rise to look at the photograph, the Inspector interposes himself between them and the photograph.

"One person and one line of enquiry at a time."

Mr Birling tells the Inspector that he fired Eva Smith because she suddenly decided to ask for more money.

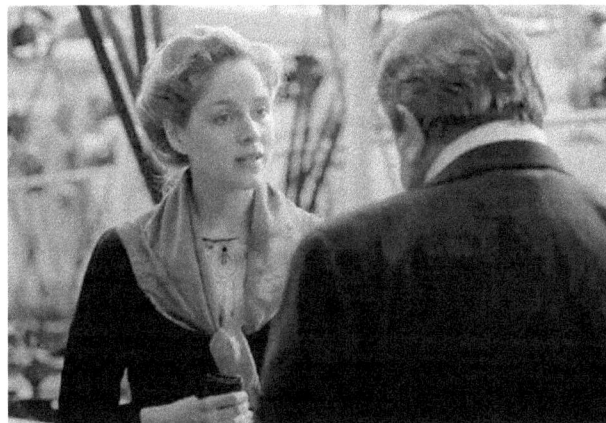

EVA SMITH being dismissed by MR BIRLING

Gerald's character is exposed here. He seems to sense that he may be involved, so he is trying to slyly sneak away.

"Wouldn't you rather I was out of it?"

Priestley exposes Mr Birling as being very power-hungry because when he introduces Gerald to the Inspector, he made it a point of mentioning Gerald's social status,

"the son of Sir George Croft – you know, Croft Limited."

Gerald: (*smiling*) I hope so.
Inspector: (*gravely*) Then I'd prefer you to stay
Gerald: (*surprised*) Oh – all right.

Birling: (*somewhat impatiently*) Look – there's nothing mysterious – or scandalous – about this business – at least not so far as I'm concerned. It's perfectly straightforward case, and as it happened more than eighteen months ago – nearly two years ago – obviously it has nothing whatever to do with the wretched girl's suicide. Eh, Inspector?
Inspector: No, sir. I can't agree with you there.
Birling: Why not?
Inspector: Because what happened to her then may have determined what happened to her afterwards, and what happened to her afterwards may have driven her to suicide. A chain of events.
Birling: Oh well – put like that, there's something in what you say. Still, I can't accept any responsibility. If we were all responsible for everything that happened to everybody we'd had anything to do with, it would be very awkward, wouldn't it?
Inspector: Very awkward.
Birling: We'd all be in an impossible position, wouldn't we?
Eric: By Jove, yes. And as you were saying, Dad, a man has to look after himself-
Birling: Yes, well, we needn't go into all that.
Inspector: Go into what?
Birling: Oh – just before you came – I'd been giving these young men a little good advice. Now – about this girl, Eva Smith. I remember her quite well now. She was a lively good-looking girl – country-bred, I fancy – and she'd been working in one of our machine shops for over a year. A good worker too. In fact, the foreman there told me he was ready to promote her into what we call a leading operator – head of a small group of girls. But after they came back from their holidays that August, they were all rather restless, and they suddenly decided to ask for more money. They were averaging about twenty-two and six, which was neither more nor less than is paid generally in our industry. They wanted the rates raised so that they could average about twenty-five shillings a week. I refused, of course.

Mr Birling is yet again impatient with the Inspector's questioning and insists that he,

"has nothing whatever to do with the wretched girl's suicide,"

showing that he is totally unconcerned and his blatant use of the adjective, 'wretched' further intensifies his cold, detached attitude towards his employees.

The Inspector tells Mr Birling that his action of firing Eva Smith had a ripple effect after that. Having been fired by him, she was forced to seek alternative employment which landed her on the streets. These chain of events, led to her suicide. Mr Birling is still unmoved, and adamant and he insists,

"Still, I can't accept any responsibility."

He further explains that,

"If we were all responsible for everything that happened to everybody we'd had anything to do with, it would be very awkward, wouldn't it?"

Once again, he expresses his selfishness.

Mr Birling acknowledges that he remembers her quite well after seeing the photograph and pressure from the Inspector. He remembers her as being a 'lively, good-looking girl', and 'a good worker too'.

Then he reveals that she and her fellow workers decided to ask for more money and he says,

"I refused, of course".

Inspector: Why?
Birling: (*surprised*) Did you say 'Why?'?
Inspector: Yes. Why did you refuse?

Birling: Well, Inspector, I don't see that it's any concern of yours how I choose to run my business. Is it now?

Inspector: It might be, you know.
Birling: I don't like that tone.
Inspector: I'm sorry. But you asked me a question.
Birling: And you asked me a question before that, a quite unnecessary question too.
Inspector: It's my duty to ask questions.

Birling: Well it's my duty to keep labour costs down. And if I'd agreed to this demand for a new rate we'd have added about twelve per cent to our labour costs. Does that satisfy you? So I refused. Said I couldn't consider it. We were paying the usual rates and if they didn't like those rates, they could go and work somewhere else. It's a free country, I told them.

Eric: It isn't if you can't go and work somewhere else.
Inspector: Quite so.
Birling: (*to Eric*) Look – just you keep out of this. You hadn't even started in the works when this happened. So they went on strike. That didn't last long, of course.
Gerald: Not if it was just after the holidays. They'd be all broke – if I know them.
Birling: Right, Gerald. They mostly were. And so was the strike, after a week or two. Pitiful affair. Well, we let them all come back – at the old rates – except the four or five ring-leaders, who'd started the trouble. I went down myself and told them to clear out. And this girl, Eva Smith, was one of them, she'd had a lot to say – far too much – so she had to go.
Gerald: You couldn't have done anything else.
Eric: He could. He could have kept her on instead of throwing her out. I call it tough luck.
Birling: Rubbish! If you don't come down sharply on some of these people, they'd soon be asking for the earth.

When the Inspector asks him why he refused, he was very rude and arrogant towards the Inspector.

"I don't see that it's any concern of yours how I choose to run my business"

Typical of the capitalist class, Mr Birling says that,

"it's my duty to keep labour costs down"

He explicitly describes how angry he was because the workers asked for more money, and they began to strike. He particularly vents his frustration towards Eva Smith, saying that,

"she'd had a lot to say – far too much – so she had to go."

Gerald is supportive and replies,

"You couldn't have done anything else."

Although Gerald agrees with Mr Birling's decision of firing Eva Smith, Eric – once again stands up to his father,

"He could have kept her on instead of throwing her out."

Eric who represents the younger generation in the play is Priestley's vision for the future. He wanted the younger generation to be responsible for the poorer social class and Eric's sense of empathy is exactly what Priestley wanted.

There is quite a challenge developing here between Mr Birling and the Inspector.

Mr Birling's ruthless character is glaring here when he says,

"If you don't come down sharply on these people, they'd soon be asking for the earth"

Gerald: I should say so!

Inspector: They might. But after all it's better to ask for the earth than to take it.

Birling: (*staring at the inspector*) What did you say your name was, Inspector?
Inspector: Google. G. double O-L-E.
Birling: How do you get on with our Chief constable, Colonel Roberts?
Inspector: I don't see much of him.

Birling: Perhaps I ought to warn you that he's an old friend of mine, and that I see him fairly frequently. We play golf together sometimes up at the West Brumley.

Inspector: (*dryly*) I don't play golf.
Birling: I didn't suppose you did.
Inspector: No, I've never wanted to play.

Eric: No, I mean about this girl – Eva Smith. Why shouldn't they try for higher wages? We try for the highest possible prices. And I don't see why she should have been sacked just because she'd a bit more spirit than the others. You said yourself she was a good worker. I'd have let her stay.

Birling: (*rather angrily*) Unless you brighten your ideas, you'll never be in a position to let anybody stay or to tell anybody to go. It's about time you learnt to face a few responsibilities. That's something this public-school-and-varsity life you've had doesn't seem to teach you.

Eric: (*sulkily*) Well, we don't need to tell the Inspector all about that, do we?
Birling: I don't see we need to tell the inspector anything more. In fact, there's nothing I can tell him. I told the girl to clear out, and she went. That's the last I heard of her. Have you any idea what happened to her after that? Get into trouble? Go on the streets?
Inspector: (*rather slowly*) No, she didn't exactly go on the streets.

END OF PART 3

The use of the adverb 'sharply' suggesting that he is superior to them and that he can control them.

Highlighting their insignificance or lack of status, as Mr Birling sees them. The Inspector gives a fitting response,

"It's better to ask for the earth than to take it"

Insinuating that Mr Birling is benefiting from Capitalism and wrongfully taking what rightfully belongs to the poor socialist class.
He also tries to show the Inspector how much influence he has when he talks about knowing the Chief Constable of police. He is also rather threatening to the Inspector when he says,

"I ought to warn you that he's an old friend of mine."

Although Eric was described as 'uneasy' but his strength is admirable because he just couldn't get over the terrible way that Eva Smith was treated and at this point he didn't know that he was involved in her death. He possessed a natural sense of empathy, something that Priestley desired in everyone.

"Why shouldn't they try for higher wages?"
"We try for the highest possible prices"
"I'd have let her stay"

His father became irate with him and told him that,

"It's about time you learnt to face a few responsibilities"

Eric is sulking because Mr Birling embarrasses him in front of the Inspector. It's quite obvious that there is a rather strained relationship between Eric and his father.

Mr Birling is furious and immediately associate Eva Smith to the streets,

"Go on the streets?"

Typical behaviour of the Capitalist towards the poor Socialist class.

START OF PART 4

EVA SMITH alias DAISY RENTON
alias Mrs BIRLING
mother of ERIC's unborn baby

//Sheila *has now entered* //

  Sheila: (*gaily*) What's this about streets? (*noticing the inspector.*) Oh – sorry. I didn't know. Mummy sent me in to ask you why you didn't come along to the drawing-room.
  Birling: We shall be along in a minute now. Just finishing.

  Inspector: I'm afraid not.

  Birling: (*abruptly*) There's nothing else, y'know. I've just told you that.
  Sheila: What's all this about?
  Birling: Nothing to do with you, Sheila. Run along.
  Inspector: No, wait a minute, Miss Birling.

  Birling: (*angrily*) Look here, Inspector, I consider this uncalled-for and officious. I've half a mind to report you. I've told you all I know – and it doesn't seem to me very important – and now there isn't the slightest reason why my daughter should be dragged into this unpleasant business.
  Sheila: (*coming father in*) What business? What's happening?

[SHEILA HAS NOW ENTERED]

SHEILA

Note the stage directions – Sheila comes in gaily but that happy mood is about to be disrupted by the Inspector's revelation. When Sheila told Mr Birling that Mrs Birling had requested their presence in the drawing room, to the annoyance of Mr Birling, the Inspector refused.

"I'm afraid not."

The Inspector asks Sheila to stay behind, and Mr Birling tells him angrily that

"it doesn't seem to me, very important"

and he should not drag Sheila,

"into this unpleasant business"

She is curious and she delves further,

"What business? What's happening."

Inspector: (*impressively*) I'm a police inspector, miss Birling. This afternoon a young woman drank some disinfectant, and died, after several hours of agony, tonight in the infirmary.

Sheila: Oh – how horrible! Was it an accident?

Inspector: No. she wanted to end her life. She felt she couldn't go on any longer.
Birling: Well, don't tell me that's because I discharged her from my employment nearly two years ago.

Eric: That might have started it.

Sheila: Did you, dad?

Birling: Yes. The girl had been causing trouble in the works. I was quite justified.

Gerald: Yes, I think you were. I know we'd have done the same thing. Don't look like that Sheila.

Sheila: (*rather distressed*) Sorry! It's just that I can't help thinking about this girl – destroying herself so horribly – and I've been so happy tonight. Oh I wish you hadn't told me. What was she like? Quite young?
Inspector: Yes. Twenty-four.
Sheila: Pretty?
Inspector: She wasn't pretty when I saw her today, but she had been pretty – very pretty.
Birling: That's enough of that.

Gerald: And I don't really see that this inquiry gets you anywhere, Inspector. It's what happened to her since she left Mr Birling's works that is important.
Birling: Obviously. I suggested that some time ago.
Gerald: And we can't help you there because we don't know.
Inspector: (*slowly*) Are you sure you don't know.

//He looks at Gerald *then at* Eric, *then at* Sheila //

When Sheila hears the news about Eva Smith's death, her response is quite different to that of Mr Birling,

"Oh – how horrible! Was it an accident?"

Her shock is seen in the effective use of punctuation. Her empathy is admirable with the audience. Sheila too is Priestley's vision for the future. He uses her to represent social responsibility and fulfilling Priestley's ideals to make the younger generation become conscious of their responsibility towards society.

Eric makes Mr Birling feel guilty because he hints that Eva's death is as a result of Mr Birling's firing of her.

"That might have started it"

Sheila is rather distressed at this news, but Mr Birling is adamant that he was justified in his decision. He shows no remorse at all.

"I was quite justified"

There is a distinct change of tone and mood in Sheila from being excited and happy to distress as seen by the stage directions. We wonder what her reaction will be like when she learns that she is also involved in Eva Smith's death. Priestley uses dramatic tension.

Gerald, although from the younger generation acts, differently to Eric and Sheila. He is more inclined to side with Mr Birling because of his wealth and social status, typical of the rich, privileged offspring of the Edwardian Era.

"Yes, I think you were. I know we'd have done the same thing"

Birling: And are you suggesting now that one of them knows something about this girl?
Inspector: Yes.

Birling: You didn't come here just to see me, then?
Inspector: No.

// the other four exchange bewildered and perturbed glances. //

Birling: (*with marked change of tone*) Well, of course, if I'd known that earlier, I wouldn't has called you officious and talked about reporting you. You understand that, don't you, Inspector? I thought that – for some reason best known to yourself – you were making the most of this tiny bit of information I could give you. I'm sorry. This makes a difference. You sure of your facts?

Inspector: Some of them – yes.
Birling: I can't think they can be of any great consequence.
Inspector: The girl's dead though.

Sheila: What do you mean by saying that? You talk as if we were responsible-

Birling: (*cutting in*) Just a minute, Sheila. Now, Inspector, perhaps you and I had better go and talk this over quietly in a corner-

Sheila: (*cutting in*) Why should you? He's finished with you. He says it's one of us now.

Birling: Yes, and I'm trying to settle it sensibly for you.

Gerald: Well, there's nothing to settle as far as I'm concerned. I've never known an Eva Smith.

Eric: Neither have I.
Sheila: Was that her name? Eva Smith?
Gerald: Yes.
Sheila: Never heard it before.

When the Inspector tells Mr Birling that he didn't only come to see him but the other members of his family as well, they exchanged 'bewildered and perturbed glances.' This shocked response can suggest their guilt about their role in Eva Smith's death.

Surprisingly, we note a marked change in Mr Birling's attitude. He is well aware that his family is involved, and he is desperate to protect them to the point of stooping to the Inspector.

"I wouldn't have called you officious and talked about reporting you"

Sheila is bewildered and she asks the Inspector,

"You talk as if we were responsible-"

Mr Birling is trying to coax the Inspector not to get his family involved,

"talk this over quietly in a corner"

Sheila's boldness is surprising because she cuts in and refuses for her father to talk in private.

"Why should you? He's finished with you."

We can juxtapose this bold utterance to that of earlier, "I am listening, daddy"

The audience is quite pleased to witness Sheila's strength and development from a shy, docile teenager to a strong woman.

Gerald oozes confidence here and tells the Inspector that he has nothing to settle regarding Eva Smith.

"I've never known an Eva Smith."

We can juxtapose his cowardly behaviour later when he finds out that he had also contributed to Daisy Renton's death.

He tried to sneak away from the room to avoid the Inspector's questioning and asked Sheila not to tell the Inspector that he knew Eva Smith.

Gerald: So where are you now, Inspector?

Inspector: Where I was before, Mr Croft. I told you – that like a lot of these young women, she'd used more than one name. She was still Eva Smith when Mr Birling sacked her – for wanting twenty-five shillings a week instead of twenty-two and six. But after that she stopped being Eva Smith. Perhaps she'd had enough of it.

Eric: Can't blame her.

Sheila: (to Birling) I think it was a mean thing to do. Perhaps that spoilt everything for her.

Birling: Rubbish! (to inspector.) Do you know what happened to this girl after she left my works?

Inspector: Yes. She was out of work for the next two months. Both her parents were dead, so that she'd no home to go back to. And she hadn't been able to save much out of what Birling and Company had paid her. So that after two months, with no work, no money coming in, and living in lodgings, with no relatives to help her, few friends, lonely, half-starved, she was feeling desperate.

Sheila: (warmly) I should think so. It's a rotten shame.

Inspector: There are a lot of young women living that sort of existence in every city and big town in this country, Miss Birling. If there weren't, the factories and warehouses wouldn't know where to look for cheap labour. Ask your father.

Sheila: But these girls aren't cheap labour – they're people.

Inspector: (dryly) I've had that notion myself from time to time. In fact, I've thought that it would do us all a bit of good if sometimes we tried to put ourselves in the place of these young women counting their pennies, in their dingy little back bedrooms.

Sheila: Yes, I expect it would. But what happened to her then?

We are going to take note of the fact that Eva Smith had three aliases, Eva Smith, Daisy Renton and Mrs Birling, that's why everyone denied knowing her because they were confused about her name.

The Inspector said that she was Eva Smith when Mr Birling sacked her. One can connote that she had a respectable job and a respectable name but after that she stopped being Eva Smith suggesting a loss of identity and dignity because later, she was forced to work on the streets under the alias Daisy Renton which Gerald and Eric recognised.

Both Sheila and Eric reprimand their father for firing Eva Smith. Sheila says,

"I think it was a mean thing to do?"

The Inspector pricks at their conscience when he 'rubs salt on their wounds ', and he tells them that she was homeless, she had no parents to help her, few friends, lonely, half-starved and desperate.
This long list from the Inspector is a deliberate ploy to make everyone feel guilty about their mistreatment towards Eva Smith.

The Inspector maps out the plight of the poor Socialist class like Eva Smith. He tells Sheila that there are many Eva Smiths living pathetic lives because of abject poverty, a sentiment he mirrors in his last speech.

"There are a lot of young women living that sort of existence in every city."

Priestley used Eva Smith to represent the poor socialist class who were taken advantage of by the rich capitalist class. Eva Smith was used, abused and discarded by Gerald and Eric.

The Inspector tells Sheila that her father uses these women as cheap labour. Sheila is horrified and she retorts,

"But these girls aren't cheap labour – they're people"

Inspector: She had what seemed to her a wonderful stroke of luck. She was taken on in a shop – and a good shop too – Milwards.

Sheila: Milwards! We go there – in fact, I was there this afternoon – (*archly to* Gerald) for your benefit.

Gerald: (*smiling*) Good!

Sheila: Yes, she was a lucky to get taken on at Milwards.

Inspector: That's what she thought. And it happened that at the beginning of December that year – nineteen-ten – there was a good deal of influenza about and Milward's suddenly found themselves short-handed. So that gave her a chance. It seems she liked working there. It was nice change from a factory. She enjoyed being among pretty clothes, I've no doubt. And now she felt she was making a good fresh start. You can imagine how she felt.

Sheila: Yes, of course.

Birling: And then she got herself into trouble there, I suppose?

Inspector: After about a couple of months, just when she felt she was settling down nicely, they told her she'd have to go.
Birling: Not doing her work properly?
Inspector: there was nothing wrong with the way she was doing her work. They admitted that.
Birling: There must have been something wrong.
Inspector: All she knew was – that a customer complained about her – and so she had to go.
Sheila: (*staring at him, agitated*) When was this?
Inspector: (*impressively*) At the end of January – last year.
Sheila: What – what did this girl look like?
Inspector: If you'll come over here, I'll show you.

Priestley creates a lot of suspense here because we are curious to see Sheila's reaction when she learns that she contributed to Eva Smith's death.

Sheila was unaware of this because she was tucked away in her position of privilege, but the Inspector had awakened in her the reality of the poor Socialist class and their struggle for survival because they are imprisoned by poverty.

The Inspector very smoothly draws Sheila into his web. He slowly reveals that Eva Smith worked at Milwards. Sheila's immediate response and innocent tone,

"Milward's! We go there,"

will turn to one of shock and horror once she learns of her role in Eva Smith's death. Priestley sets the tone and pace for us and creates much suspense and tension.
The Inspector is, "beating around the bush," with unnecessary details of how Eva Smith was employed by Milward's, as though he is deliberately dragging out Sheila's agony and he seems to be enjoying her pain.

"She enjoyed being among pretty clothes"
"she felt she was making a good fresh start. You can imagine how she felt."

Note Mr Birling's rude interruptions,

"And then she got herself into trouble there"

Earlier he said that she was a good worker and now he accuses her of not doing her work properly.
Typical behaviour of the Capitalist class employer and his disregard for his employee, which annoyed the Inspector.

The Inspector made it quite clear that she was a good worker, but Mr Birling still insisted that Eva Smith had done something wrong. His attitude towards the poor working class can mirror Mrs Birling attitude, "Women of that sort."

TEXT ACT 1 part 4	EXPLANATION
// He moves nearer a light – perhaps standard lamp – and she crosses to him. He produces the photograph. She looks at it closely, recognizes it with a little cry, gives a half-stifled sob, and then runs out. The inspector puts the photograph back in his pocket and stares speculatively after her. The other three stare in amazement for a moment. //	They clearly look down upon the poor Socialist class. The Inspector's long drawn explanation about Eva Smith's employment at Milward's reaches a climax when Sheila realises that she had Eva Smith fired.

Priestley creates a lot of suspense and tension because he wants us to see her reaction compared to that of her parents.
The Inspector uses various techniques to create a dramatic impact, for example, he moves closer to the light and only shows the photograph to Sheila. By the use of light imagery one can imply that the Inspector is bringing light into Sheila's life.
Her reaction gets an emotive response from the audience because she displayed empathy and remorse for what she has done.

Eric, Gerald, and Sheila all deny knowing Eva Smith. This is because she uses different names like Eva Smith, Daisy Renton, and Mrs Birling. Let us look at the irony of these names. Eva Smith somewhat transcended the barrier from the poor socialist class to the rich capitalist class because she was carrying Eric's child.

Sadly, Mrs Birling cut that possibility short by refusing to give her financial help because she called herself Mrs Birling. Priestley is showing us how the rich ensured that the poor could not transcend the boundary between the rich and poor.

The Inspector was very sarcastic when he delivers a very emotive speech about how many women like Eva Smith from the poor socialist class were desperate, hungry and helpless without jobs or money.

When the Inspector shows her the photograph, Sheila recognises it and,

"with a little cry, gives a half-stifled sob, and then runs out." |

Birling: What's the matter with her?	Mr Birling asks,
Eric: She recognized her from the photograph, didn't she?	"What's the matter with her"
Inspector: Yes.	Mr Birling stares at the Inspector angrily and blames him for spoiling his nice little family celebration,
Birling: (angrily) Why the devil do you want to go upsetting the child like that?	Mr Birling is furious with the Inspector for upsetting Sheila because he is protective of his family,
Inspector: I didn't do it. She's upsetting herself.	"Why the devil do you want to go upsetting the child like that?"
Birling: Well – why – why?	
Inspector: I don't know – yet. That's something I have to find out.	Note that Mr Birling calls Sheila a 'child', yet she is a grown woman, but Sheila starts developing into a strong woman after this.
Birling: (still angrily) Well – if you don't mind – I'll find out first.	
Gerald: Shall I go after her.	The Inspector responds beautifully by reminding Mr Birling that he went to the Infirmary, and he says that,
Birling: (moving) No, leave this to me. I must also have a word with my wife – tell her what's happening. (turns at the door, staring at the inspector angrily.) We were having a nice family celebration tonight. And a nasty mess you've made of it now, haven't you?	"a nasty mess somebody's made of it"
	Referring to Eva Smith's body. The Inspector tries to target Mr Birling's conscience. He presents him with a graphic, visual and violent description of Eva Smith's dead body. In so doing he hopes that this visual imagery will elicit an emotive, empathetic response from Mr Birling. Unfortunately, he very coldly exits, showing no empathy or remorse.
Inspector: (steadily) That's more or less what I was thinking earlier tonight when I was in the infirmary looking at what was left of Eva Smith. A nice little promising life there, I thought, and a nasty mess somebody's made of it.	
// Birling looks as if about to make some retort, then thinks better of it, and goes out, closing door sharply behind him. Gerald and Eric exchange uneasy glances. The Inspector ignores them. //	'closing the door sharply behind him'
	In conclusion, Priestley has drawn the audience's attention to the disparity between privileged class women like Sheila who got rich men to marry and were taken care of by their husbands and those underprivileged women like Eva Smith who had to work hard to survive and take care of not only themselves but their families in the unjust Edwardian society.
END OF PART 4	

START OF PART 5

Gerald: I'd like to have a look at that photograph now, Inspector.

Inspector: All in good time.
Gerald: I don't see why -
Inspector: (*cutting in, massively*) You heard what I said before, Mr Croft. One line of inquiry at a time. Otherwise we'll all be taking at once and won't know where we are. If you've anything to tell me, you'll have an opportunity of doing it soon.

Gerald: (*rather uneasily*) Well, I don't suppose I have –
Eric: (*suddenly bursting out*) Look here, I've had enough of this.
Inspector: (*dryly*) I dare say.
Eric: (*uneasily*) I'm sorry – but you see – we were having a little party – and I've had a few drinks, including rather a lot of champagne – and I've got a headache – and as I'm only in the way here – I think I'd better turn in.
Inspector: And I think you'd better stay here.
Eric: Why should I?
Inspector: It might be less trouble. If you turn in, you might have to turn out again soon.
Gerald: Getting a bit heavy-handed, aren't you, inspector?
Inspector: Possibly. But if you're easy with me, I'm easy with you.

Gerald: After all, y'know, we're respectable citizens and not criminals.

Inspector: Sometimes there isn't much difference as you think. Often, if it was left to me, I wouldn't know where to draw the line.

Gerald: Fortunately, it isn't left to you, is it?
Inspector: No, it isn't. But some things are left to me. Inquiries of this sort, for instance.

//Enter Sheila, *who looks as if she's been crying*//
Well, Miss Birling?

[GERALD AND THE INSPECTOR]

Gerald becomes impatient and asks the Inspector whether he can see the photograph, but the Inspector does not relent,

"All in good time"

Gerald's response here is very hypocritical because he said,

"I don't see why -"

The rich had a lot of 'skeletons in their cupboard.' A classic example, apart from Gerald is Alderman Meggarty who displayed some vile behaviour with Eva Smith.

The Inspector is very firm with Gerald. He is organised and systemic and tells Gerald,

"One line of enquiry at a time."

This unnerves Gerald and he is 'rather uneasy'. He tells the Inspector,

"we're respectable citizens and not criminals"

Of course, we know that Gerald is not what he appears to be. He is hiding under a false cloak of respectability. He is displaying a superficial façade because he also had an affair with Eva Smith. The Inspector sarcastically says that,

"I wouldn't know where to draw the line"

[ENTER SHIELA]

Sheila: (*coming in, closing the door*) You knew it was me all the time, didn't you?

Inspector: I had an idea it might be – from something the girl herself wrote.

Sheila: I've told my father – he didn't seem to think it amounted to much – but I felt rotten about it at the time and now I feel a lot worse. Did it make much difference to her?

Inspector: Yes, I'm afraid it did. It was the last real steady job she had. When she lost it – for no reason that she could discover – she decided she might as well try another kind of life.

Sheila: (*miserably*) So I'm really responsible?

Inspector: No, not entirely. A good deal happened to her after that. But you're partly to blame. Just as your father is.

Eric: But what did Sheila do?

Sheila: (*distressed*) I went to the manager at Milward's and I told him that if they didn't get rid of that girl, I'd never go near the place again and I'd persuade mother to close our account with them.

Inspector: And why did you do that?

Sheila: Because I was in a furious temper.

Inspector: And what had this girl done to make you lose your temper?

Sheila: When I was looking at myself in the mirror, I caught sight of her smiling at the assistant, and I was furious with her. I'd been in a bad temper anyhow.

Inspector: And was it the girl's fault?

Sheila: No, not really. It was my own fault. (*suddenly, to* Gerald) All right, Gerald, you needn't look at me like that. At least, I'm trying to tell the truth. I expect you've done things you're ashamed of too.

Gerald: (*surprised*) Well, I never said I hadn't. I don't see why –

inspector:(*cutting in*) Never mind about that. You can settle that between you afterwards. (*to* Sheila.) What happened?

Sheila tells the Inspector that she told her father, and his response was that,

"he didn't seem to think it amounted to much."

Once again, Mr Birling's selfishness is highlighted but Sheila's response is different, it's one of empathy,

"but I felt rotten about it at the time and now I feel a lot worse"

We have to note how the different generations react differently. The older generation is cold and detached and do not accept responsibility, whilst the younger generation are sympathetic, and they accept responsibility – something that Priestley envisioned.

The Inspector pricks Sheila's conscience and reminds her that Eva Smith got fired because of her, and out of desperation,

"she decided she might as well try another kind of life"

Sheila's response is really admirable, she is 'miserable' and she accepts responsibility unlike her parents,

"So I'm really responsible?"

the Inspector is rather blunt, and he targets her conscience,

"But you're partly to blame"

Sheila explains how she got Eva Smith fired. She went to the manager at Milward's and told him that if he didn't get rid of Eva Smith, she would persuade her mother to close her account there. Sheila even admits that,

"It was my own fault"

Sheila: I'd gone in to try something on. It was an idea of my own – mother had been against it, and so had the assistant – but I insisted. As soon as I tried it on, I knew they'd been right. It just didn't suit me at all. I looked silly in the thing. Well, this girl had brought the dress up from the workroom, and when the assistant – Miss Francis – had asked her something about it, this girl, to show us what she meant, had held the dress up, as if she was wearing it. And it just suited her. She was the right type for it, just as I was the wrong type. She was very pretty too – with big dark eyes – and that didn't make it any better. Well, when I tried the thing on and looked at myself and knew that it was all wrong, I caught sight of this girl smiling at miss Francis – as if to say: 'doesn't she look awful' – and I was absolutely furious. I was very rude to both of them, and then I went to the manager and told him that this girl had been very impertinent – and – and– (*she almost breaks down, but just controls herself.*)

How could I know what would happen afterwards? If she'd been some miserable plain little creature, I don't suppose I'd have done it. But she was very pretty and looked as if she could take care of herself. I couldn't be sorry for her.

Inspector: In fact, in a kind of way, you might be said to have been jealous of her.

Sheila: Yes, I suppose so.

Inspector: And so you used the power you had, as a daughter of a good customer and also of a man well known in the town, to punish the girl just because she made you feel like that?

Sheila: Yes, but it didn't seem to be anything very terrible at the time. Don't you understand? And if I could help her now, I would-

Inspector:(*harshly*) Yes, but you can't. It's too late. She's dead.

Eric: My god, it's a bit thick, when you come to think of it-

SHEILA – SYBIL – EVA SMITH alias DAISY

Sheila's frank and honest explanation, as she detailed the events that led to Eva Smith's dismissal is quite endearing.

"I looked silly in this thing"
"And It just suited her"
"She was the right type"

She also admits that Eva Smith

"was very pretty too - with big dark eyes"

and that she was also jealous because the dress suited her so well. She feels so remorseful that she wishes if she could help her now, but the Inspector very harshly says that,

"it's too late. She's dead."

We tend to forgive her shortfalls because of the empathy she showed and her genuine, deep sense of remorse.

Sheila: (*stormily*) Oh shut up, Eric. I know I know. It's the only time I've ever done anything like that, and I'll never, never do it again to anybody. I've noticed them giving me a sort of look sometimes at Milwards – I noticed it even this afternoon – and I suppose some of them remember. I feel now I can never go there again. Oh – why had this to happen?

Inspector: (*sternly*) That's what I asked myself tonight when I was looking at that dead girl. And then I said to myself: 'well, we'll try to understand why it had to happen?' and that's why I'm here, and why I'm, not going until I know all that happened. Eva Smith lost her job with Birling and company because the strike failed and they were determined not to have another one. At last she found another job – under what name I don't know – in a big shop, and had to leave there because you were annoyed with yourself and passed the annoyance on to her. Now she had to try something else. So first she changed her name to Daisy Renton-

Gerald: (*startled*) What?

Inspector: (*steadily*) I said she changed her name to Daisy Renton.

Gerald: (*pulling himself together*) D'you mind if I give myself a drink, Sheila?

// Sheila *merely nods, still staring at him, and he goes across to the tantalus on the sideboard for a whisky.* //

Inspector: Where is your father, Miss Birling?

Sheila: He went into the drawing room, to tell mother what was happening here. Eric, take the inspector along to the drawing-room.

// As Eric *moves, the inspector looks from* Sheila *to* Gerald, *then goes out with Eric.* //

Well, Gerald?

Gerald: (*trying to smile*) Well what, Sheila?

Sheila: How did you come to know this girl – Eva Smith?

Gerald: I didn't.

Sheila: Daisy Renton then – it's the same thing.

Gerald: Why should I have to known her?

We see that Sheila is now maturing and taking responsibility for her actions once again. Her redeeming qualities can make us understand her indiscretion with Eva Smith because she says,

"Oh – why had this to happen?"

When the Inspector explains the terrible events that led to Eva Smith's death. He tells them that she had changed her name to Daisy Renton and Gerald became immediately startled and involuntarily blurted out,

"What?"

The Inspector repeats the name,

"I said she changed her name to Daisy Renton"

Stunned, Gerald, pulls himself together while Sheila stares at him, and seeks permission from Sheila to get a drink,

"D'you mind if I give myself a drink, Sheila?"

The Inspector see an opportunity to leave Sheila and Gerald to their own devices to discuss Gerald's relationship with Eva Smith alias Daisy Renton by asking Sheila,

"Where is your father, Miss Birling?"

Sheila directs Eric to take the Inspector along to the drawing room.

The Inspector leaves the room with Eric, leaving Sheila and Gerald to themselves.

Sheila: Oh don't be stupid. We haven't much time. You gave yourself away as soon as he mentioned her other name.

Gerald: All right. I knew her. Let's leave it at that.

Sheila: We can't leave it at that.

Gerald: (*approaching her*) Now listen, darling-

Sheila: no, that's no use. You not only knew her but you knew her very well. Otherwise, you wouldn't look so guilty about it. When did you first get to know her?

// he does not reply//

Was it after she left Milwards? When she changed her name, as he said, and began to lead a different sort of life? Were you seeing her last spring and summer, during that time you hardly came near me and said you were so busy? Were you?

// he does not reply but looks at her //

Yes, of course you were.

Gerald: I'm sorry, Sheila. But it was all over and done with, last summer. I hadn't set eyes on the girl for at least six months. I don't come into this suicide business.

Sheila: I thought I didn't half an hour ago.

Gerald: You don't. Neither of us does. So – for God's sake – don't say anything to the inspector.

Sheila: About you and this girl?

Gerald: Yes. We can keep it from him.

Sheila: (*laughs rather hysterically*) Why – you fool – he knows. Of course he knows. And I hate to think how much he knows that we don't know yet. You'll see. You'll see.

// *she looks at him almost in triumph. He looks crushed. The doors slowly opens and the* Inspector *appears, looking steadily and searchingly at them.* //

Inspector: Well?

END OF PART 5

          END OF ACT ONE

Sheila questions Gerald about his association with Eva Smith but he vehemently denies knowing her – of course he is lying once again. Then he finally admits to knowing her. She asks him if he was seeing her all last Summer. He apologises to her but says,

"I don't come into this suicide business"

He is trying divorce himself from the situation. He also doesn't want Sheila to tell the Inspector about him and Eva Smith. Priestley uses dramatic irony here because the audience already knows that the Inspector is aware of Gerald's involvement.

Sheila laughs at Gerald and calls him a fool and tells him that the Inspector already knows. The Inspector comes back in.

This indicates that he deliberately left them to themselves to have an argument about Gerald's affair with Eva Smith. The Inspector is very clever in his techniques – he looks steadily and searchingly at them to gage their reaction.

[INSPECTOR GOOLE QUESTIONS SHEILA AND GERALD]

The tension at the end of Act 1 continues to the beginning of Act 2 because the Inspector deliberately left Sheila and Gerald along to quarrel among themselves. He comes back with a "Well?" Priestley creates a lot of suspense here because we want to see Gerald's reaction to the Inspector's questioning in the presence of Sheila. He does not want to reveal details of the affair in front of Sheila and he asks her to leave but she's adamant and she refuses to go. He thinks that Sheila wants to revel in his misery. They both began to bicker and Sheila thinks that Gerald now views her as being a

>"selfish, vindictive creature"

Because of her terrible treatment of Eva Smith. However, the Inspector 'massively takes charge' and tells Gerald that Sheila wants to stay and hear otherwise,

>"she'll feel she's entirely to blame,
>
>she'll be alone with her responsibility."

The Inspector tells them very sternly,

>"We'll have to share our guilt"

- A message echoed from Priestley's socialist ideals.

[MRS BIRLING ENTERS]

Mrs Birling enters briskly with an air of self-confidence. She is totally unaware of what is happening. Smiling and with an easy tone she greets and introduces herself to the inspector. She tells him very blatantly,

>"I don't think we can help you much."

And Sheila begs her to stop,

>"No, mother – please!"

But Mrs Birling ignores her and tells the Inspector that he's had a huge impact on Sheila,

>"made a great impression on Sheila."

We can gage that Sheila is heeding the Inspector and she is quite fascinated at his mysterious manner, and she warns her mother that the Inspector will break down any walls that she builds between Eva Smith and them. She also warns her mother that,

>"She is beginning all wrong."

Mrs Birling learns of Eric's heavy drinking from Sheila and Gerald, but she is in total denial. Even later after Eric confesses that while he was drunk, he got Eva Smith pregnant, she still says that he doesn't drink very much.

[MR BIRLING ENTERS]

He is irate that he couldn't get Eric to go to bed. The Inspector wants to question him. Mr Birling is treating Eric like a little child. At this point both Mr and Mrs Birling are furious with the Inspector for his intrusion on their happy lives. Mr Birling says,

> "I don't propose to give you much more rope."

Gerald very sneakily denies ever knowing Eva Smith, but Sheila's goading and the Inspector's intuition forces him to confess. He then outlines in detail how he met Eva Smith at the Palace Bar, bought her food, found her lodgings, gave her money and had an affair with her. He is visibly shaken about her death and goes out to take a walk. But before he goes Sheila interrupts him and hands him his engagement ring, saying that they,

> "aren't the same people who sat down to dinner here."

[GERALD EXITS]

Priestley creates suspense and tension when the Inspector shows the photograph of Eva Smith only to Mrs birling who pretends not to recognise Eva Smith. The Inspector accuses her of lying and tells her,

> "You're not telling me the truth."

Surprisingly, Sheila agrees with the Inspector, and she too accuses her mother of not telling the truth. Both Mr and Mrs Birling are outraged and demand an apology from the Inspector who boldly refuses, saying that he is merely doing his duty. Entrances and Exits are important in this play because it causes much tension and suspense, and it helps to move the plot along.

[ERIC EXITS]

The Inspector tells Mr and Mrs Birling that Eric must return to answer some questions, otherwise he will go and find him, to the bewilderment of Mr and Mrs Birling.

After a little deliberation, Mrs Birling admits that she met Eva Smith two weeks earlier. She was desperate and came for some assistance to the Brumley Women's Charity Organisation, of which Mrs Birling chairs and has the authority of who to turn down for help and in this case – Eva Smith. She is furious that Eva Smith dared to call herself 'Mrs Birling' which she thought as being rather 'impertinent'. She also says that they help, 'deserving' people.

We witness first hand Mrs Birling's hypocrisy – typical of the Capitalist class of the Edwardian era. I mean who was more deserving than Eva Smith. Priestley writes with a bitter tone when describing Mrs Birling here and her sense of arrogance and superiority is quite unnerving to the audience who view her attitude as distasteful and they tend to empathise with Eva Smith's predicament.

Mrs Birling refuses to accept responsibility for her behaviour and says that Eva Smith,
     "Only had herself to blame,"
And, of course, the father of the child should take responsibility and he
     "ought to be dealt with very severely."
Mrs Birling also tells the Inspector that Eva Smith said that she turned down the money that Eric offered her because it was stolen. Of course, Mrs Birling refused to believe that a woman of her poor social standing would embark on something as moral as that. To Mrs Birling, however, the poor socialist class lacked morals and dignity.
     "Girls of that class."

[ERIC ENTERS PALE AND DISTRESSED]

START OF PART 6

// *At rise, scene and situation are exactly as they were at end of Act one. The INSPECTOR remains at the door for a few moments looking at SHEILA and GERALD. Then he comes forward, leaving door open behind him.* //

Inspector: (*To Gerald*) Well?
Sheila: (*with hysterical laugh, to Gerald*) You see? What did I tell you?
Inspector: What did you tell him?

Gerald: (*with an effort*) Inspector, I think Miss Birling ought to be excused any more of this questioning. She'd nothing more to tell you. She's had a long exciting and tiring day – we were celebrating our engagement, you know – and now she's obviously had about as much as she can stand. You heard her.

Sheila: He means that I'm getting hysterical now.
Inspector: And are you?
Sheila: Probably.
Inspector: Well, I don't want to keep you here. I've no more questions to ask you.
Sheila: No, but you haven't finished asking questions – have you?
Inspector: No.

Sheila: (to Gerald) You see? (to Inspector.) then I'm staying.

Gerald: Why should you? It's bound to be unpleasant and disturbing.

Inspector: And you think young women ought to be protected against unpleasant and disturbing things?

Gerald: If possible – yes.

[GERALD AND THE INSPECTOR]

GERALD CROFT

Gerald doesn't want Sheila to hear about his sordid affair with Eva Smith. He knows that the Inspector is going to reveal all, so he is desperate to spare Sheila the details.

He pleads to the Inspector to let her be excused.

"I think Miss Birling ought to be excused any more of this questioning"

We see Sheila's fast development here because she insists on staying,

"then I'm staying."

Gerald tells her that,

"It's bound to be unpleasant and disturbing."

Once again, the Inspector delivers a scathing attack when he asks Gerald,

"And you think young women ought to be protected against unpleasant and disturbing things?"

Inspector: Well, we know one young woman who wasn't, don't we?

Gerald: I suppose I asked for that.
Sheila: Be careful you don't ask for more, Gerald.
Gerald: I only meant to say to you – Why stay when you'll hate it?
Sheila: It can't be any worse for me than it has been. And it might be better.
Gerald: (*bitterly*) I see.
Sheila: What do you see?
Gerald: You've been through it – and now you want to see somebody else put through it.

Sheila: (*bitterly*) So that's what you think I'm really like. I'm glad I realized it in time, Gerald.

Gerald: No, no, I didn't mean -
Sheila: (*cutting in*) Yes, you did. And if you'd really loved me, you couldn't have said that. You listened to that nice story about me. I got that girl sacked from Milward's. And now you've made up your mind I must obviously be a selfish, vindictive creature.
Gerald: I neither said that nor even suggested it.
Sheila: Then why say I want to see somebody else put through it? That's not what I meant at all.
Gerald: All right then, I'm sorry.
Sheila: Yes, but you don't believe me. And this is just the wrong time not to believe me.

Inspector: (*massively taking charge*) Allow me, Miss Birling. (to Gerald.) I can tell you why Miss Birling wants to stay on and why she says it might be better for her if she did. A girl died tonight. A pretty, lively sort of girl, who never did anybody any harm. But she died in misery and agony – hating life –

Sheila: (*distressed*) Don't please – I know, I know – and I can't stop thinking about it –

Gerald said that he thinks that they should, and the Inspector shamed him by saying,

"We know one woman who wasn't, don't we?"

INSPECTOR GOOLE - SHEILA

The stage directions state that both Sheila and Gerald speak 'bitterly' this portrays the tension and anger between them.

Gerald accuses Sheila of deriving pleasure from his misery because she was put through the same misery by the Inspector.

Sheila is annoyed with Gerald for saying that,

"So that's what you think I'm really like"

At this point Sheila becomes very depressed and argumentative with Gerald. The Inspector gives her a violent, graphic imagery of how Eva Smith died,

"But she died in misery and agony – hating life -"

Sheila is very distressed and asks the Inspector to stop torturing her,

"Don't please – I know, I know – and I can't stop thinking about it -"

Inspector: *(ignoring this)* Now Miss Birling has just been made to understand what she did to this girl. She feels responsible. And if she leaves us now, and doesn't hear any more, then she'll feel she's entirely to blame, she'll be alone with her responsibility, the rest of tonight, all tomorrow, all the next night--

Sheila: *(eagerly)* Yes, that's it. And I know I'm to blame – and I'm desperately sorry – but I can't believe – I won't believe – it's simply my fault that in that in the end she – she committed suicide. That would be too horrible –

Inspector: *(sternly to them both)* You see, we have to share something. If there's nothing else, we'll have to share our guilt.

Sheila: *(staring at him)* Yes. That's true. You know. *(she goes close to him, wonderingly.)* I don't understand about you.

Inspector: *(calmly)* There's no reason why you should.

END OF PART 6

She stops and her sentence is incomplete, and one can infer that she stopped to visualise the terrible scene of Eva Smith's death. The Inspector tugs at Sheila's conscience and she says that,

"She feels responsible"

The Inspector talks sternly to them and tells them that they will,

"have to share our guilt"

START OF PART 7

// He regards her calmly while she stares at him wonderingly and dubiously. Now Mrs Birling enters, briskly and self-confidently, quite out of key with the little scene that has just passed. Sheila feels this at once. //

<u>Mrs Birling</u>: (*smiling social*) Good evening Inspector.
<u>Inspector</u>: Good evening, madam.

<u>Mrs Birling</u>: (*same easy tone*) I'm Mrs Birling, y'know. My husband has just explained why you're here, and while we'll be glad to tell you anything you want to know, I don't think we can help you much.

<u>Sheila</u>: No, Mother – please!

<u>Mrs Birling</u>: (*affecting great surprise*) What's the matter, Sheila?
<u>Sheila</u>:(*hesitantly*) I know it sounds silly--
<u>Mrs Birling</u>: What does?

<u>Sheila</u>: You see, I feel you're beginning all wrong. And I'm afraid you'll say or do something that you'll be sorry for afterwards.

<u>Mrs Birling</u>: I don't know what you're talking about, Sheila.

<u>Sheila</u>: We all started like that – so confident, so pleased with ourselves until he began asking us questions.

// Mrs Birling looks from Sheila to the Inspector. //

<u>Mrs Birling</u>: You seem to have made a great impression on this child, Inspector.
<u>Inspector</u>: (*coolly*) we often do on the young ones. They're more impressionable.

// He and Mrs Birling look at each other for a moment. Then Mrs Birling turns to Sheila again //

Mrs Birling comes in with an easy tone and arrogant attitude and tells the Inspector,

"I don't think we can help you much"

Sheila is aghast and she urges her mother,

"No, Mother – please!"

and she tells her mother that she feels that,

"you're beginning all wrong"

Sheila also foreshadows her mother's behaviour because she warns her,

"you'll say or do something that you'll be sorry for afterwards."

And, of course, Mrs Birling does regret her utterances later on when she discovers that Eric is the father of Eva Smith's child.

Sheila explains to her mother that,

"We all started like that – so confident, so pleased with ourselves until he began asking us questions"

Mrs Birling: You're looking tired, dear. I think you ought to go to bed – and forget about this absurd business. You'll feel better in the morning.

Sheila: Mother, I couldn't possibly go. Nothing could be worse for me. We've settled all that. I'm staying here until I know why that girl killed herself.
Mrs Birling: Nothing but morbid curiosity.
Sheila: No it isn't.

Mrs Birling: Please don't contradict me like that. And in any case I don't suppose for a moment that we can understand why the girl committed suicide. Girls of that class-

Sheila:(*urgently, cutting in*) Mother, don't – please don't. For your own sake, as well as ours, you mustn't-

Mrs Birling: (*annoyed*) Mustn't – What? Really, Sheila!

Sheila: (*slowly, carefully now*) You mustn't try to build up a kind of wall between us and that girl. If you do, then the Inspector will just break it down. And it'll be all the worse when he does.

Mrs Birling: I don't understand you. (*to Inspector.*) Do you?
Inspector: Yes. And she'd right.
Mrs Birling: (*haughtily*) I beg your pardon!
Inspector: (*very plainly*) I said yes – I do understand her. And she's right.
Mrs Birling: that – I consider – is a trifle impertinent, Inspector.

// *Sheila gives short hysterical laugh* //

now, what is it, Sheila?

Sheila: I don't know. Perhaps it's because impertinent is such a silly word.

Mrs Birling: In any case....

Mrs Birling wants Sheila to go to bed and forget all,

"about this absurd business"

Sheila is adamant and strong. She stands up to her mother expressing her desire to stay until she knows, 'why the girl killed herself'. Sheila is wracked with guilt. Mrs Birling uses euphuism when she says,

"Girls of that class-"

It is a very demeaning thing to say. Her coldness shocks the audience. Her reaction, being of the older generation, she behaves in the classic capitalist manner of being very cold and detached. Once again, Sheila urgently pleads to her mother,

"don't, please don't, for your own sake, as well as ours, you mustn't –"

Sheila is so desperate to stop her mother that she once again abruptly ends her sentence showing her desperation.

Mrs Birling brushes Sheila off and she becomes annoyed with Sheila,

"Mustn't – What? Really Sheila!"

Slowly, carefully, Sheila responds,

"You mustn't try to build up a kind of wall between us and that girl"

Sheila is warning her mother of the Inspector's power. It's ironical because this is the very wall between the Capitalist and Socialist classes that Priestley envisioned breaking down and Sheila is trying to break that wall down. She goes on to say that,

"the Inspector will just break it down"

The Inspector represents the conscience of the people. We can say that he represents Priestley's ideals, and the Inspector is here to conscientize the Birlings about social responsibility,

"And it'll be all the worse when he does"

Sheila: But, Mother, do stop before it's too late.

Mrs Birling: If you mean that the inspector will take offence-

inspector: (*cutting in, calmly*) No, no. I never take offence.

Mrs Birling: I'm glad to hear it. Though I must add that it seems to me that we have more reason for taking offence.

Inspector: Let's leave offence out of it, shall we?

Gerald: I think we'd better.

Sheila: So do I.

Mrs Birling: (*rebuking them*) I'm talking to the inspector now, if you don't mind. (*to Inspector, rather grandly*.) I realise that you may have to conduct some sort of inquiry, but I must say that so far you seem to be conducting it in a rather peculiar and offensive manner. You know of course that my husband was Lord Mayor only two years ago and that he's still a magistrate-

Gerald: (*cutting, rather impatiently*) Mrs Birling, the Inspector knows all that. And I don't think it's a very good idea to remind him-

Sheila: (*cutting in*) It's crazy. Stop it, please, Mother.

Inspector: (*imperturbable*) Yes. Now what about Mr Birling?

Mrs Birling: He's coming back in a moment. He's just talking to my son, Eric, who seems to be in an excitable silly mood.

Inspector: What's the matter with him?

Instead of carrying on with Gerald's confession in Act 2, Priestley creates suspense because he puts it on hold and moves the action to Mrs Birling and Sheila. Knowing Mrs Birling's character, the audience is also curious about Mrs Birling's reaction to Gerald's involvement in Eva Smith's death.

Mrs Birling is a social snob, and her arrogance is glaring here when she accuses the Inspector of being impertinent. Sheila scoffs at her mother's attitude by laughing hysterically and declaring that the word impertinent is such a silly word and her mother shouldn't use it. Sheila is getting increasingly desperate and urges her mother to stop,

"But, Mother do stop before it's too late"

We will draw a juxtaposition between Mrs Birling's rude demeanour here to later in the play when she learns that Eric is the father of Eva Smith's child. Here she has an unstoppable air of confidence and pride. Her behaviour is rather grand when she accuses the Inspector of conducting his enquiry,

"in a rather peculiar and offensive manner"

She also tries to threaten the Inspector into submission,

"my husband was Lord Mayor only two years ago, and he's still a magistrate."

By now Gerald is quite alarmed at Mrs Birling's attitude and he cuts in rather impatiently causing her to leave her sentence unfinished hanging in mid-air. Even Gerald now understands the Inspector's powers and he too urges her to stop,

"I don't think it's a very good idea to remind him-"

Even Sheila, in all her desperation cuts in again and asks her mother to stop it,

"It's crazy. Stop it, please, Mother."

Mrs Birling: Eric? Oh – I'm afraid he may have had rather too much to drink tonight. We were having a little celebration here--

inspector: (*cutting in*) Isn't he used to drinking?

Mrs Birling: No, of course not. He's only a boy.

Inspector: No, he's a young man. And some young men drink far too much.
Sheila: And Eric's one of them.
Mrs Birling: (*very sharply*) Sheila!

Sheila:(*urgently*) I don't want to get poor Eric into trouble. He's probably in enough trouble already. But we really must stop these silly pretences. This isn't the time to pretend that Eric isn't used to drink. He's been steadily drinking too much for the last two years.

Mrs Birling: (*staggered*) it isn't true. You know him, Gerald -and you're a man – you must know it isn't true.

Inspector:(*as Gerald hesitates*) Well, Mr Croft?
Gerald: (*apologetically, to* Mrs Birling) I'm afraid it is, y'know. Actually I've never seen much of him outside this house – but- well, I have gathered that he does drink pretty hard.
Mrs Birling: (*bitterly*) And this is the time you choose to tell me.
Sheila: Yes, of course it is. That's what I meant when I talked about building up a wall that's sure to be knocked flat. It makes it all harder to bear.
Mrs Birling: But it's you – and not the inspector here – who's doing it--

Sheila: Yes, but don't you see? He hasn't started on you yet.
Mrs Birling: (*after a pause, recovering herself*) If necessary I shall be glad to answer any questions the inspector wishes to ask me. Though naturally I don't know anything about this girl.
Inspector: (*gravely*) We'll see, Mrs Birling.

END OF PART 7

We see how detached Mrs Birling is with Eric. She seems to be in total denial about his drinking.

"he may have had rather too much to drink tonight"

The Inspector queries Eric's drinking 'habits',

"Isn't he used to drinking"

Mrs Birling's prompt reply is,

"No, of course not. He's only a boy."

Notice how the Birling's treat their grown-up children, like kids. Mr Birling refers to Sheila as 'child' and now Mrs Birling calls Eric a 'boy'. Shield is engaged and Eric was in the throes of fatherhood. Once again, we see Sheila's steady development into maturity. She is forthright in saying that,

"This isn't the time to pretend that Eric isn't used to drink"

Mrs Birling is 'staggered' and is still denying it,

"It isn't true"

The way Priestley presents Mrs Birling at the beginning as naïve is quite interesting because it arouses the audience's curiously, and a lot of tension is created. We are curious to see her reactions later on about Gerald's and her and Eric's involvement with Eva Smith's death.

At this point in the play, Sheila seemed to have swayed towards the Inspector's side. She tells her mother that the Inspector,

"hasn't started on you yet"

Mrs Birling's demeanour had now changed markedly, and she agrees to co-operate with the Inspector,

"I shall be glad to answer any questions the Inspector wishes to ask me"

START OF PART 8

// enter birling, who closes door behind him //

Birling: (*rather hot, bothered*) I've been trying to persuade Eric to go to bed, but he won't. Now he says you told him to stay up. Did you?

Inspector: Yes, I did.
Birling: Why?
Inspector: Because I shall want to talk to him, Mr Birling.
Birling: I can't see why you should, but if you must, then I suggest you do it now. Have him in and get it over, then let the lad go.
Inspector: No, I can't do that yet. I'm sorry, but he'll have to wait.
Birling: Now look here, Inspector--

Inspector: (*cutting in, with authority*) He must wait his turn.

Sheila: (*to Mrs Birling*) You see?

Mrs Birling: No, I don't. And please be quiet, Sheila.

Birling: (*angrily*) Inspector, I've told you before, I don't like the tone nor the way you're handling this inquiry. And I don't propose to give you much rope.

Inspector: You needn't give me any rope.

Sheila: (*rather wildly, with laugh*) No, he's giving us the rope – so that we'll hang ourselves.

Birling: (*to Mrs Birling*) What's the matter with that child?
Mrs Birling: Over-excited. And she refuses to go. (*with sudden anger, to* Inspector.) Well, come along – what is it you want to know?

[ENTER MR BIRLING]

Once again, we are shocked at how the Birlings treat Eric and Sheila as though they were little kids.

"I've been trying to persuade Eric to go to bed, but he won't. Now he says you told him to stay up. Did you?"

The Inspector asserts his authority here when he tells Mr Birling that Eric has to,

"wait his turn"

The Inspector manages to set the 'cat among the pigeons' because there is much tension between the Birlings. Mrs Birling gets angry with Sheila when she points out the Inspector's authority,

"You see?"

Mrs Birling is furious and she responds,

"No, I don't. And please be quiet, Sheila."

Priestley uses a rope imagery which is symbolic of hanging and death – Mrs Birling says'

"I don't propose to give you much more rope."

Sheila laughs rather wildly and tells her parents that it's the Inspector who is giving them the rope,

"So, we'll hang ourselves."

We note the shock response from Mr and Mrs Birling when the Inspector questions Gerald about knowing Eva Smith. Of course, Gerald once again, attempted to deny it but Sheila cuts him short saying,

Inspector: (*coolly*) at the end of January, last year, this girl Eva Smith had to leave Milwards, because Miss Birling compelled them to discharge her, and then she stopped being Eva Smith, looking for a job, and became Daisy Renton, with other ideas. (*sharply turning on him*.) Mr Croft, when did you first get to know her?

// *An exclamation of surprise from birling and Mrs Birling.* //

Gerald: Where did you get the idea that I did know her?
Sheila: It's no use, Gerald. You're wasting time.

Inspector: As soon as I mentioned the name Daisy Renton, it was obvious you'd known her. You gave yourself away at once.
Sheila: (*bitterly*) Of course he did.
Inspector: And anyhow I knew already. When and where did you first meet her?
Gerald: All right, if you must have it. I met her first, sometime in March last year, in the stalls bar at the Palace. I mean the Palace music hall here in Brumley-

Sheila: Well, we didn't think you meant Buckingham Palace.

Gerald: (*to* Sheila) Thanks. You're going to be a great help, I can see. You've said your piece, and you're obviously going to hate this, so why on earth don't you leave us to it?

Sheila: Nothing would induce me. I want to understand exactly what happens when a man says he's so busy at the works that he can hardly ever find time to come and see the girl he's supposed to be in love with. I wouldn't miss it for worlds-

Inspector: (*with authority*) Yes, Mr Croft – in the stalls bar at the Palace Variety Theatre.
Gerald: I happened to look in, one night, after a long dull day, and as the show wasn't very bright, I went down into the bar for a drink. It's a favourite haunt of women of the town-

"It's no use, Gerald. You're wasting time."

There is a huge change in Sheila's disposition. We see a steady development into maturity from a carefree, happy girl to now a bitter, strong woman. Priestley adds a sense of humour to cut the tension when Sheila says,

"Well, we didn't think you meant Buckingham Palace"

when Gerald said that he met Eva Smith at the 'Palace Music Hall'. Sheila's strength and bitterness is evident here with Gerald's infidelity.

Sheila reminiscences about earlier in the play when Gerald lied to her. He told her that he was working all Summer but in fact he was seeing Eva Smith. Sheila is mature enough now to understand exactly how Gerald lies and pretends, hence her throwing the ring at him and her refusal to take it back.

GERALD with EVA SMITH alias DAISY RENTON

Gerald asks Sheila to leave but she displays an unusual strength and determination when she refuses to go,

"I wouldn't miss it for world."

Gerald uses the euphemism,

"women of the town-"

Mrs Birling: Women of the town?

Birling: Yes, yes. But I see no point in mentioning the subject – especially - (*indicating* Sheila.)

Mrs Birling: It would be much better if Sheila didn't listen to this story at all.

Sheila: But you're forgetting I'm supposed to be engaged to the hero of it. Go on, Gerald. You went down into the bar, which is a favourite haunt of the women of the town.

Gerald: I'm glad I amuse you-

Inspector: (*sharply*) Come along, Mr Croft. What happened?

Gerald: I didn't propose to stay long down there. I hate those hard-eyed dough-faced women. But then I noticed a girl who looked quite different. She was very pretty – soft brown hair and big dark eyes- (*breaks off*.) My god!

Inspector: What's the matter?

Gerald: (*distressed*) Sorry – I – well, I've suddenly realized – taken it in properly – that's she's dead-

Inspector: (*harshly*) Yes, she's dead.

Sheila: And probably between us we killed her.

Mrs Birling: (*sharply*) Sheila, don't talk nonsense.

Sheila: You wait, Mother.

Inspector: (*to* Gerald) Go on.

Gerald: She looked young and fresh and charming and altogether out of place down here. And obviously she wasn't enjoying herself. Old Joe Meggarty, half-drunk and goggle-eyed, had wedged her into a corner with that obscene fat carcass of his-

Mrs Birling: (*cutting in*) There's no need to be disgusting. And surely you don't mean Alderman Meggarty?

Gerald: Of course I do. He's a notorious womanizer as well as being one of the worst sots and rogues in Brumley--

Inspector: Quite right.

Mrs Birling: (*staggered*) Well, really! Alderman Meggarty! I must say, we are learning something tonight.

Mrs Birling's reaction is one of utter shock and she repeats what Gerald had said,

"Women of the town?"

Gerald is very distressed at this point when he explains how he met Eva Smith, then he suddenly realised that she is dead.

Priestley's continuous use of the hyphens suggests that Gerald is struggling to contain his emotions.

"Sorry – I – well, I've suddenly realized – taken it properly – that's she's dead-"

Sheila then adds,

"And probably between us we killed her."

To which Mrs Birling responds furiously,

"Sheila, don't talk nonsense."

Gerald reveals how Old Joe Meggarty had Eva Smith wedged into a corner but Mrs Birling cuts in and asks Gerald whether he means Aldermen Meggarty. Mrs Birling is staggered to hear that Joe Meggarty is a notorious womaniser,

"Well, really! Alderman Meggarty!"

ALDERMAN JOE MEGGARTY with EVA SMITH

Sheila: (*coolly*) of course we are. But everybody knows about that horrible old Meggarty. A girl I know had to see him at the Town Hall one afternoon and she only escaped with a torn blouse-

Birling: (*sharply, shocked*) Sheila!

Inspector: (*to* Gerald) Go on, please.

Gerald: The girl saw me looking at her and then gave me a glance that was nothing less than a cry for help. So I went across and told Joe Meggarty some nonsense – that the manager had a message for him or something like that – got him out of the way – and then told the girl that if she didn't want any more of that sort of thing, she'd better let me take her out of there. She agreed at once.

Inspector: Where did you go?

Gerald: We went along to the County Hotel, which I knew would be quiet at that time of night, and we had a drink or two and talked.

Inspector: Did she drink much at the time?

Gerald: No. She only had a port and lemonade – or some such concoction. All she wanted was to talk – a little friendliness – and I gathered that Joe Meggarty's advances had left her rather shaken – as well they might-

Inspector: She talked about herself?

Gerald: Yes. I asked her questions about herself. She told me her name was Daisy Renton, that she'd lost both parents, that she came originally from somewhere outside Brumley. She also told me she'd had a job in one of the works here and had had to leave after a strike. She said something about the shop too, but wouldn't say which it was, and she was deliberately vague about what happened. I couldn't get any exact details from her about herself – just because she felt I was interested and friendly – but at the same time she wanted to be Daisy Renton – and not Eva Smith.

In fact, I heard that name for the first time tonight. What she did let slip – though she didn't mean to – was that she was desperately hard up and at that moment was actually hungry. I made the people at the county find some food for her.

Inspector: And then you decided to keep her – as your mistress?

The repeated exclamation marks can denote Mrs Birling's shock and surprise.

Here Priestley is hitting out at the Capitalist class of the Edwardian society who had 'Skeletons' in their cupboards, and yet pretended to be upright citizens of Society. Gerald is a classic example. Meggarty and Gerald are upstanding members of the Capitalist society yet both of them indulged in clandestine love affairs with Eva Smith. Mrs Birling's shock at Meggarty's misbehaviour highlights this.

Gerald details his relationship with Eva Smith.
Eva Smith poured out her heart to him and told him that she had lost both parents, she lost her job after a strike and was vague about being fired from Milwards.

She also revealed to him that she was hungry and that she was desperately hard up so he ordered some food for her.

The inspector curtly asks him,

"And you decided to keep her – as your mistress?"

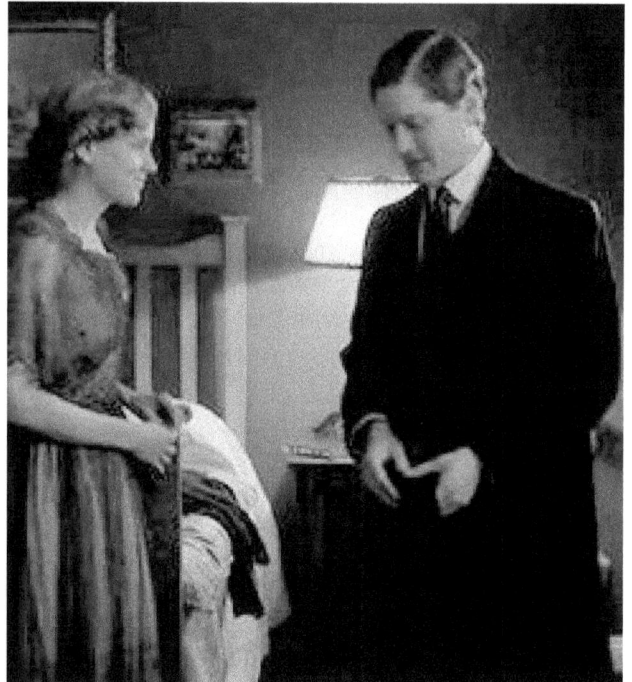

EVA SMITH with GERALD at the FLAT

<u>Mrs Birling:</u> What?

<u>Sheila:</u> Of course, Mother. It was obvious from the start. Go on, Gerald. Don't mind mother.

<u>Gerald:</u> (*steadily*) I discovered, not that night but two nights later, when we met again – not accidentally this time of course - that in fact she hadn't a penny and was going to be turned out of the miserable back room she had. It happened that a friend of mine, Charlie Brunswick, had gone off to Canada for six months and had let me have the key of a nice little set of rooms he had – in Morgan Terrace – and had asked me to keep an eye on them for him and use them if I wanted to. So I insisted on Daisy moving into those rooms and I made her take some money to keep her going there. (*carefully, to the Inspector.*) I want you to understand that I didn't install her there so that I could make love to her. I made her go to Morgan Terrace because I was sorry for her and didn't like the idea of her going back to the Palace bar. I didn't ask for anything in return.

<u>Inspector:</u> I see.

<u>Sheila:</u> Yes, but why are you saying that to him? You ought to be saying it to me.

<u>Gerald:</u> I suppose I ought really. I'm sorry, Sheila. Somehow I-
<u>Sheila:</u> (*cutting in, as he hesitates*) I know. Somehow he makes you.
<u>Inspector:</u> But she became your mistress?
<u>Gerald:</u> Yes. I suppose it was inevitable. She was young and pretty and warm hearted – and intensely grateful. I became at once the most important person in her life – you understand?
<u>Inspector:</u> Yes. She was a woman. She was lonely. Were you in love with her?
<u>Sheila:</u> just what I was going to ask!

Mrs Birling replied with a shocked

"What?"

Sheila's tone of sarcasm reveals her anger and her maturity because she urges Gerald to reveal details of his relationship with Eva Smith.

"Go on, Gerald."

The Inspector and Sheila grill Gerald about his affair with Eva Smith.

Gerald reveals how Eva Smith was about to be thrown out of,

"the miserable back room she had"

so he gave her some money and tries to convince the Inspector that,

"I didn't install her there so that I could make love to her"

He felt sorry for her and didn't want her to go back to the Palace bar.

Sheila: "Yes, but why are you saying that to him? You ought to be saying it to me"

We become aware of Sheila's fascination with the Inspector because she is beginning to act like him with all her grilling questions,

"I know. Somehow he makes you."

The inspector's direct question,

"But she became your mistress?"

is sure to unnerve and embarrass Gerald. We now see a very humiliated, forlorn Gerald and not the confident 'Man about town'.

He talks positively about Eva Smith saying that she was,

"pretty and warm hearted – and intensely grateful"

TEXT	EXPLANATION

Birling: (*angrily*) I really must protest-

Inspector: (*turning on him sharply*) Why should you do any protesting? It was you who turned the girl out in the first place.

Birling: (*rather taken aback*) Well, I only did what any employer might have done. And what I was in which my daughter, a young unmarried girl, is being dragged into this-

inspector: (*sharply*) Your daughter isn't living on the moon. She's here in Brumley too.
Sheila: Yes, and it was I who had the girl turned out of her job at Milwards. And I'm supposed to be engaged to Gerald. And I'm not a child, don't forget. I've a right to know. Were you in love with her, Gerald?
Gerald: (*hesitatingly*) It's hard to say. I didn't feel about her as she felt about me.
Sheila: (*with sharp sarcasm*) Of course not. You were the wonderful Fairy Prince. You must have adored it, Gerald.
Gerald: All right – I did for a time. Nearly any man would have done.
Sheila: That's probably about the best thing you've said tonight. At least it's honest. Did you go and see her every night?
Gerald: No. I wasn't telling you a complete lie when I said I'd been very busy at the works all that time. We were very busy. But of course I did see a good deal of her.

Mrs Birling: I don't think we want any further details of this disgusting affair-

Sheila: (*cutting in*) I do. And anyhow, we haven't had any details yet.
Gerald: And you're not going to have any. (*to Mrs Birling.*)
You know, it wasn't disgusting.
Mrs Birling: It's disgusting to me.
Sheila: Yes, but after all, you didn't come into this, did you, Mother?
Gerald: Is there anything else you want to know – that you ought to know?
Inspector: Yes. When did this affair end?

I think that despite the fact that Gerald made love to Eva Smith we tend to forgive him and excuse his behaviour because he showed genuine concern and helped Eva Smith in her time of need albeit for only a short while.
At this point Mr Birling is furious,

"I really must protest."

But the Inspector turned on him sharply and pointed out that he was responsible for Eva Smith's pathetic situation by firing her.

"It was you who turned the girl out in the first place"

Mr Birling is very concerned about protecting his family. He is furious that Sheila is being exposed to all this adult talk.

"a young unmarried girl, is being dragged into this"

Once again, we see Sheila treated as a child but this time she stands up to her father,

"And I'm not a child, don't forget"

Once again, we see Sheila's maturity and development as compared to her response to her father earlier in the play.

"Daddy I am listening"

Sheila is adamant that she waits to hear details of Gerald's sordid affair despite Mrs Birling saying,

"I don't think we want any further details of this disgusting affair."

Gerald stands up to Mrs Birling when she says that the affair was disgusting,

"You know, it wasn't disgusting"

This sentiment somewhat endears Gerald to the audience.

TEXT ACT 2 part 8	EXPLANATION
Gerald: I can tell you exactly. In the first week of September. I had to go away for several weeks then – on business – and by that time Daisy knew it was coming to an end. So I broke it off definitely before I went. Inspector: How did she take it? Gerald: Better than I'd hoped. She was – very gallant – about it. Sheila: (*with irony*) That was nice for you. Gerald: No, it wasn't. (*he waits a moment, then in a low, troubled tone.*) She told me she'd been happier than she'd ever been before – but that she knew it couldn't last – hadn't expected it to last. She didn't blame me at all. I wish to God she had now. Perhaps I'd feel better about it. Inspector: She had to move out of those rooms? Gerald: Yes, we'd agreed about that. She'd saved a little money during the summer – she'd lived very economically on what I'd allowed her – and didn't want to take more from me, but I insisted on a parting gift of enough money – though it wasn't so very much – to see her through to the end of the year. Inspector: Did she tell you what she proposed to do after you'd left her? Gerald: No. she refused to talk about that. I got the idea, once or twice from what she said, that she thought of leaving Brumley. Whether she did or not – I don't know. Did she? Inspector: Yes. She went away for about two months. To some seaside place. Gerald: By herself? Inspector: Yes. I think she went away – to be alone, to be quiet, to remember all that had happened between you. Gerald: How do you know that? Inspector: She kept a rough sort of diary. And she said there that she had to go away and be quiet and remember ' just to make it last longer'. She felt there'd never be anything as good again for her – so she had to make it last longer.	Gerald tells the Inspector that he ended the affair with Eva Smith when he had to go away on business. "She was very - gallant - about it." Note the use of hyphens used by Gerald suggesting his nervousness and embarrassment because his speech does not flow. Priestley tells us that Gerald had a 'low, troubled tone' suggesting that he is wracked with guilt about Eva Smith's death and his shoddy treatment of her. He has regrets and wished to God that she had blamed him so he would have felt, " I wish to God she had now. Perhaps I'd feel better about it" His use of the biblical imagery suggest that he is genuinely remorseful about his actions, but we have to juxtapose it to his nonchalant attitude in the end when he discovered that the Inspector wasn't 'real.' Typical of the capitalist classes inconsiderate behaviour, he forgot about Eva Smith's death and resumed his normal lifestyle. The Inspector tells Gerald that Eva Smith left Brumley, and Gerald's response is one of concern, "By herself" The Inspector then pricks at his conscience, and he tells Gerald that Eva Smith went away, "to remember all that had happened between you" Hence instilling in Gerald, a guilty conscience. The Inspector told Gerald that Eva Smith kept a diary and in it she wrote that she wanted to make the memory of her affair with Gerald last longer. "she said there that that she had to go away and be quiet and remember"

Gerald: (*gravely*) I see. Well, I never saw her again, and that's all I can tell you.

Inspector: It's all I want to know from you.

Gerald: In that case – as I'm rather more – upset – by this business than I probably appear to be – and – well, I'd like to be alone for a while – I'd be glad if you'd let me go.

Inspector: Go were? Home?

Gerald: No. I'll just go out – walk about – for a while, if you don't mind. I'll come back.

Inspector: All right, Mr Croft.

Sheila: But just in case you forget – or decide not to come back, Gerald, I think you'd better take this with you. (*she hands him the ring.*)

Gerald: I see. Well, I was expecting this.

Sheila: I don't dislike you as I did half an hour ago, Gerald. In fact, in some odd way, I rather respect you more than I've ever done before. I knew anyhow you were lying about those months last year when you hardly came near me. I knew there was something fishy about that time. And now at least you've been honest. And I believe what you told us about the way you helped her at first. Just out of pity. And it was my fault really that she was so desperate when you first met her. But this has made a difference. You and I aren't the same people who sat down to dinner here. We'd have to start all over again, getting to know each other-

Birling: Now, Sheila, I'm not defending him. But you must understand that a lot of young men-

Sheila: Don't interfere, please, Father. Gerald knows what I mean, and you apparently don't.

Gerald: Yes, I know what you mean. But I'm coming back – if I may.

Sheila: All right.

Mrs Birling: Well, really, I don't know. I think we've just about come to an end of this wretched business-

Gerald: I don't think so. Excuse me.

// He goes out. They watch him go in silence. We hear the front door slam. //

END OF PART 8

Exits and entrances are important in the play. Now Gerald exits to clear his troubled mind. It seems that the Inspector's questioning is having a great impact on Gerald and the Birlings thus far. Gerald's exit is symbolic as well because Sheila gives him back the ring before he leaves. We can assume that Sheila's and Gerald's union is more of a business transaction rather than real love because despite what Gerald did
Mr Birling makes excuses for him.

"But you must understand that a lot of young men."

Sheila promptly tells her father,

"Don't interfere, please, Father."

Sheila's strength of character and her development is once highlighted as she boldly stands up to her father. Now she is not listening to her father like the docile girl in Act 1.

"I am listening, daddy."

In Edwardian times, we must note that if women married into a wealthy family, their lives and their social status were secured as in this case Sheila marrying Gerald.

Gerald leaves and Mrs Birling is well relieved and thinks this whole affair regarding Eva Smith is over.

"I think we've just about come to the end of this wretched business"

But Gerald is very perceptive when he replies.

"I don't think so"

START OF PART 9

Sheila: (*to* Inspector) You know, you never showed him that photograph of her.

Inspector: No. it wasn't necessary. And I thought it better not to.

Mrs Birling: You have a photograph of this girl?

Inspector: Yes. I think you'd better look at it.

Mrs Birling: I don't see any particular reason why I should-

Inspector: Probably not. But you'd better look at it.

Mrs Birling: Very well. (*he produces the photograph and she looks hard at it.*)

inspector: (*taking back the photograph*) you recognize her?

Mrs Birling: No. Why should I?

Inspector: Of course she might have changed lately, but I can't believe she could have changed so much.

Mrs Birling: I don't understand you, Inspector.

Inspector: You mean you don't choose to do, Mrs Birling.

Mrs Birling: (*angrily*) I meant what I said.

Inspector: You're not telling me the truth.

Mrs Birling: I beg your pardon!

Birling: (*angrily, to* Inspector) Look here, I'm not going to have this, Inspector. You'll apologize at once.

Inspector: Apologise for what – doing my duty?

Birling: No, for being so offensive about it. I'm a public man-

Inspector: (*massively*) Public men, Mr Birling, have responsibilities as well as privileges.

Birling: Possibly. But you weren't asked to come here to talk to me about my responsibilities.

[MRS BIRLING AND THE INSPECTOR]

GOOLE shows SYBIL BIRLING the photograph

Mrs Birling refuses to look at the photo of Eva Smith,

"I don't see any particular reason why I should."

ARTHUR and SYBIL furious with GOOLE

Both Mr and Mrs Birling are furious when the Inspector says,

"You mean you don't choose to do, Mrs Birling."

Mr Birling threatens the Inspector by saying that,

"I am a public man,"

To which the Inspector promptly replies,

"Public men, Mr Birling, have responsibilities as well as privileges"

Sheila: Let's hope not. Though I'm beginning to wonder.
Mrs Birling: Does that mean anything, Sheila?

Sheila: It means that we've no excuse now for putting on airs and that if we've any sense we won't try. Father threw this girl out because she asked for decent wages. I went and pushed her farther out, right into the street, just because I was angry and she was pretty. Gerald set her up as his mistress and then dropped her when it suited him. And now you're pretending you don't recognize her from that photograph. I admit I don't know why you should, but I know jolly well you did in fact recognize her, from the way you looked. And if you're not telling the truth, why should the Inspector apologize? And can't you see, both of you, you're making it worse?

// she turns away. We hear the front door slam again. //

Birling: That was the door again.
Mrs Birling: Gerald must have come back.
Inspector: Unless your son has just gone out.
Birling: I'll see.

// He goes out quickly. Inspector turns to Mrs Birling. //

Inspector: Mrs Birling, you're a member – a prominent member – of the Brumley Women's Charity Organization, aren't you?

// Mrs Birling does not reply. //

Sheila: Go on, Mother. You might as well admit it. (to Inspector.) Yes, she id. Why?
Inspector: (calmly) It's an organization to which women in distress can appeal for help in various forms. Isn't that so?
Mrs Birling: (with dignity) Yes. We've done a great deal of useful work in helping deserving cases.
Inspector: There was a meeting of the interviewing committee two weeks ago?
Mrs Birling: I dare say there was.

Sheila tells her parents,

"we've no excuse for putting on airs"

She accuses her Mother of pretending not to know Eva Smith.

"but I know jolly well you did in fact recognise her, from the way you looked"

She is trying to make her parents see reason and stop pretending. Sheila, we can say, fully understands the Inspector's role, and she defends the Inspector,

"And if you are telling the truth, why should the Inspector apologise?"

EVA SMITH interviewed by MRS BIRLING

We have to note how Priestley's use of entrances and exits creates suspense amongst the audience. It's a deliberate ploy to transfix the audience and arouse their curiosity about who is entering and exiting and the nail-biting events that follow.
Sheila has now fully developed and she is very bravely helping the Inspector when she insists that her mother answers the inspector's questions.

"Go on, Mother. You might as well admit it."

Ironically, Mrs Birling's answer to the Inspector was,

"Yes. We've done a great deal of work in helping deserving cases."

Inspector: You know very well there was, Mrs Birling. You were in the chair.

Mrs Birling: and if I was, what business is it of yours?
Inspector: (*severely*) do you want me to tell you – in plain words?

// enter birling, looking rather agitated. //

Birling: That must have been Eric.
Mrs Birling: (*alarmed*) Have you been up to his room?
Birling: Yes. And I called out on both landings. It must have been Eric we heard go out then.
Mrs Birling: Silly boy! Where can he have gone to?
Birling: I can't imagine. But he was in one of his excitable queer moods, and even though we don't need him here-
Inspector: (*cutting in, sharply*) We do need him here. And if he's not back soon, I shall have to go and find him.

// Birling and Mrs Birling exchange bewildered and rather frightened glances. //

Sheila: He's probably just gone to cool off. He'll be back soon.
Inspector: (*severely*) I hope so.
Mrs Birling: And why should you hope so?
Inspector: I'll explain why when you've answered my questions, Mrs Birling.
Birling: Is there any reason why my wife should answer questions from you, Inspector?
Inspector: Yes, a very good reason. You'll remember that Mr Croft told us – quite truthfully, I believe – that he hadn't spoken to or seen Eva smith since last September. But Mrs Birling spoke to and saw her only two weeks ago.
Sheila: (*astonished*) Mother!
Birling: Is this true?
Mrs Birling: (*after a pause*) Yes, quite true.
Inspector: She appealed to your organization for help?
Mrs Birling: Yes.
Inspector: Not as Eva Smith?
Mrs Birling: No, nor as Daisy Renton.

Mrs Birling's hypocrisy and snobbery is evident here because she refused to help Eva Smith when Eva used the name Mrs Birling. Mrs Birling wouldn't accept the fact that Eva Smith, from a lower social status will use her name.

[ENTER MR BIRLING]

Mr Birling comes in rather agitated because he can't find Eric. Mrs Birling calls Eric,

"Silly boy!"

She treats him as though he is a child and we also learn that she too is rather distanced from her son because she didn't even know about his drinking habits.

Mr Birling is very confident that Eric is not needed to be questioned until the Inspector cuts in sharply and says,

"we do need him here-"

The Inspector's firm and confident attitude is sure to shock the Birlings when he says,

"And if he's not back soon, I shall have to go and find him"

In the stage directions we see that the once confident Birlings are now

'bewildered and rather frightened'

We can compare them to the 'sunken titanic' now. All fallen and scared and powerless against the might of the Inspector. When the Inspector reveals that Mrs Birling spoke to Eva Smith, Sheila was astonished and retorts,

"Mother!"

The exclamation mark can denote Sheila's shock at her mother's involvement.

Inspector: As what then?

Mrs Birling: First, she called herself Mrs Birling--

Birling: (*astounded*) Mrs Birling!

Mrs Birling: Yes, I think it was simply a piece of gross impertinence – quite deliberate – and naturally that was one of the things that prejudiced me against her case.

Birling: And I should think so! Damned impudence!

Inspector: You admit being prejudiced against her case?

Mrs Birling: Yes.

Sheila: Mother, she's just died a horrible death – don't forget.

Mrs Birling: I'm very sorry. But I think she had only herself to blame.

Inspector: Was it owing to your influence, as the most prominent member of the committee, that help was refused the girl?

Mrs Birling: Possibly.

Inspector: Was it or was it not your influence?

Mrs Birling: (*stung*) Yes, it was. I didn't like her manner. She'd impertinently made use of our name, though she pretended afterwards it just happened to be the first she thought of. She had to admit, after I began questioning her, that she had no claim to the name, that she wasn't married, and that the story she told at first – about a husband who'd deserted her – was quite false. It didn't take me long to get the truth – or some of the truth – out of her.

Inspector: Why did she want help?

Mrs Birling: You know very well why she wanted help.

Inspector: No, I don't. I know why she needed help. But as I wasn't there, I don't know what she asked from your committee.

Mrs Birling: I don't think we need discuss it.

Inspector: You have no hope of not discussing it, Mrs Birling.

Mrs Birling very sheepishly reveals her reason for turning down Eva Smith's plea for help when she called herself Mrs Birling. Note the Capitalist response of both Mr and Mrs Birling, Mr Birling was astounded,

"Mrs Birling!"

Once again, the exclamation mark suggesting his shock. Whilst Mrs Birling called it,

"a piece of gross impertinence"

which prejudiced her against helping Eva Smith.

Mr Birling further responds,

"And I should think so! Damned impudence!"

The repeated use of the exclamation mark by Priestley can connote Mr Birling's fury.

When Mrs Birling admitted that she was prejudiced against Eva Smith, Sheila was horrified,

"Mother, she's just died a horrible death –
Don't forget"

Mrs Birling's cold and detached response shocks the audience,

"she had only herself to blame."

The Inspector tries to target her conscience and accuses her of contributing to Eva Smith's death by insisting that Mrs Birling's influence was responsible for the request of help to be turned down. Although she admitted it, Mrs Birling was unmoved to sympathise with Eva Smith's plight.

TEXT ACT 2 part 9	EXPLANATION
Mrs Birling: If you think you can bring any pressure to bear upon me, Inspector, you're quite mistaken. Unlike the other three, I did nothing I'm ashamed of or that won't bear investigation. The girl asked for assistance. We were asked to look carefully into the claims made upon us. I wasn't satisfied with the girl's claim – she seemed to me not a good case – and so I used my influence to have it refused. And in spite of what's happened to the girl since, I consider I did my duty so if I prefer not to discuss it any further, you have no power to make me change my mind. **Inspector**: Yes I have. **Mrs Birling**: No you haven't. Simply because I've done nothing wrong – and you know it. **Inspector**: (*very deliberately*) I think you did something terribly wrong – and that you're going to spend the rest of your life regretting it. I wish you'd been with me tonight in the infirmary. You'd have seen- **Sheila**: (*bursting in*) No, no, please! Not that again. I've imagined it enough already. **Inspector**: (*very deliberately*) Then the next time you imagine it, just remember that this girl was going to have a child. **Sheila**: (*horrified*) No! Oh – horrible – horrible! How could she have wanted to kill herself? **Inspector**: Because she'd been turned out and turned down too many times. This was the end. **Sheila**: Mother, you must have known. **Inspector**: It was because she was going to have a child that she went for assistance to your mother's committee. **Birling**: Look here, this wasn't Gerald Croft- **Inspector**: (*cutting in, sharply*) No, no. Nothing to do with him. **Sheila**: Thank goodness for that! Though I don't know why I should care now. **Inspector**: (*to Mrs Birling*) And you've nothing further to tell me, eh?	She is quite bold and arrogant and refuses to answer any more of the Inspector's questions, "If you think you can bring any pressure to bear upon me, Inspector, you're quite mistaken." She still insists that she did nothing wrong to be ashamed of and "– she seemed to me not a good case –" Priestley uses very many hyphens to break up Mrs Birling's speech, this can suggest that she is being careful not to incriminate herself further, hence she is carefully choosing her words. "– she seemed to me not a good case – " One will wonder what is a better case than a desperate young, pregnant girl on the streets appealing for help. Mrs Birling's standoffish attitude is sure to shock the audience and create a great deal of bitterness for her. Priestley puts on display the very core of the unacceptable attitude and prejudices of the Capitalist class of the Edwardian Era, which he so desperately wanted to put right. Priestley writes with a bitter tone about unwavering Mrs Birling who insist, despite the death of the girl that, "I've done nothing wrong -" The Inspector insists that Mrs Birling, "I think you did something terribly wrong -" and he tries to justify this by trying to paint a visual, graphic picture of Eva Smith's dead body in order to elicit a response from the cold, unfeeling Mrs Birling, when Sheila desperately bursts in, "No, no, please! Not that again. I've imagined it enough already." The Inspector very deliberately reveals that Eva Smith was pregnant, and he was able to elicit a very emotive, positive response from Sheila, "No! Oh – horrible - horrible!"

Mrs Birling: I'll tell you what I told her. Go and look for the father of the child. It's his responsibility.

Inspector: That doesn't make it any the less yours. She came to you for help, at a time when no woman could have needed it more. And you not only refused it yourself but saw to it that the others refused it too. She was here alone, friendless, almost penniless, desperate. She needed not only money but advice, sympathy, friendliness. You've had children. You must have known what she was feeling. And you slammed the door in her face.

Sheila: (*with feeling*) Mother, I think it was cruel and vile.

Birling: (*dubiously*) I must say, Sybil, that when this comes out at the inquest, it isn't going to do us much good. The Press might easily take it up--

Mrs Birling: (*agitated now*) Oh, stop it, both of you. And please remember before you start accusing me of anything again that it wasn't I who had her turned out of her employment – which probably began it all.
(*turning to Inspector.*) In the circumstances I think I was justified. The girl had begun by telling us a pack of lies. Afterwards, when I got at the truth, I discovered that she knew who the father was, she was quite certain about that, and so I told her it was her business to make him responsible. If he refused to marry her – and in my opinion he ought to be compelled to – then he must at least support, her.
Inspector: And what did she reply to that?
Mrs Birling: Oh – a lot of silly nonsense!
Inspector: What was it?

We have to once again draw a juxtaposition between the response between the rock-hard older generation and the younger generation who ooze warmth and empathy as Priestley intended them to be in order to bring light into the Edwardian ailing, fractured society.

Sheila is relieved that Gerald is not the father of Eva Smith's child and Priestly creates a lot of suspense here because we are curious as to who the father is. Mrs Birling had no qualms in saying to Eva Smith,

"Go and look for the father of the child. It's his responsibility."

The Inspector renders a scathing attack on Mrs Birling in a very poignant speech echoing Priestley's message of Social responsibility. He pointed out that it was Mrs Birling's responsibility to help Eva Smith and very emotively draws out a detailed list with the hope of getting Mrs Birling to show some sympathetic emotions. He tells her that Eva Smith was alone, penniless and desperate, that she needed advice and friendship but Mrs Birling,

"slammed the door in her face"

Sheila was disgusted with her mother's behaviour and slammed it as,

"cruel and vile"

whilst Mr Birling was more concerned about his reputation and status instead of his wife's indiscretion and cruelty towards a dead girl.

"The Press might easily take it up—"

Mrs Birling hits out at Mr Birling and Sheila and reminds them that she, wasn't the one who got Eva Smith fired and that it was their actions which got the ball rolling, which ultimately culminated in Eva Smith's death. She then denies her involvement,

"In the circumstances I think I was justified."

Mrs Birling: Whatever it was, I know it made me finally lose all patience with her. She was giving herself ridiculous airs. She was claiming elaborate fine feelings and scruples that were simply absurd in a girl in her position.

Inspector: (*very sternly*) Her position now is that she lies with a burnt-out inside on a slab. (*As Birling tries to protest, turns on him.*) Don't stammer and yammer at me again, man. I'm losing all patience with you people. What did she say?

Mrs Birling: (*rather cowed*) She said that the father was only a youngster – silly and wild and drinking too much. There couldn't be any question of marrying him – it would be wrong for them both. He had given her money but she didn't want to take any more money from him.

Inspector: Why didn't she want to take and more money from him?

Mrs Birling: All a lot of nonsense – I didn't believe a word of it.

Inspector: I'm not asking you if you believed it. I want to know what she said. Why didn't she want to take any more money from this boy?

Mrs Birling: Oh – she had some fancy reason. As if a girl of that sort would ever refuse money!

Inspector: (*sternly*) I warn you, you're making in worse for yourself. What reason did she give for not taking any more money?

Mrs Birling: Her story was – that he'd said something one night, when he was drunk, that gave her the idea that it wasn't his money.

Inspector: Where had he got it from then?

Mrs Birling: He'd stolen it.

Inspector: So she'd come to you for assistance because she didn't want to take stolen money?

Mrs Birling said that she insisted that Eva Smith make the father responsible, and that he ought to support her. The Inspector then plodded her on to reveal more details.

According to Mrs Birling Eva Smith was giving herself her airs, and that she was,

"claiming elaborate, fine feelings and scruples that were simply absurd in a girl in her position"

Mrs Birling uses euphuism to describe Eva Smith. According to her opinion it is unfathomable that a girl from a poor social background can have any morals and integrity. Only the rich was supposed to show these qualities.

Things get heated up now when the Inspector deliberately once again creates a violent, graphic picture of Eva Smiths dead body to target the Birling's conscience,

"she lies with a burnt-out inside on a slab"

Mr Birling tries to protest but the Inspector is very forceful in his approach and his rising fury is seen in this rhyme,

"Don't stammer and yammer at me again, man. I am losing all patience with you people."

Then Mrs Birling explains how Eva Smith refused the money offered to her by the child's father but of course to Mrs Birling this is strange coming from a poor girl, and she once uses euphuism to degrade Eva Smith,

"As if a girl of that sort would ever refuse money!"

The Inspector is now losing patience with Mrs Birling's arrogant attitude,

"I warn you, you're making it worse for yourself"

Mrs Birling then reveals to the Inspector that Eva Smith refused to take stolen money and the Inspector shows his disgust for Mrs Birling's indifferent attitude,

"So she'd come to you for assistance because she didn't want to take stolen money?"

TEXT ACT 2 part 9	EXPLANATION
Mrs Birling: That's the story she finally told, after I'd refused to believe her original story – that she was a married woman who'd deserted by her husband. I didn't see any reason to believe that one story should be any truer than the other. Therefore, you're quite wrong to suppose I shall regret what I did.	Mrs Birling is adamant that if Eva Smith lied one time she may lie again and that she saw no reason to believe her. And she firmly believes that her actions are justified. She is adamant right to the very end that she is right.
Inspector: But if her story was true, if this boy had been giving her stolen money, then she came to you for help because she wanted to keep this youngster out of any more trouble – isn't that so?	"Therefore, you're quite wrong to suppose that I shall regret what I did." She once again insists that she was,
Mrs Birling: Possibly. But it sounded ridiculous to me. So I was perfectly justified in advising my committee not to allow her claim for assistance.	"perfectly justified in advising my committee not to allow her claim for assistance" The Inspector is appalled at this incredulous claim and questions Mrs Birling's indifference.
Inspector: You're not even sorry now, when you know what happened to the girl?	"You're not even sorry now, when you know what happened to the girl?"
Mrs Birling: I'm sorry she should have come to such a horrible end. But I accept no blame for it at all.	Mrs Birling's ice-cold response shocks both the audience and the Inspector when she denies any responsibility for her vile actions.,
Inspector: Who is to blame then? Mrs Birling: First, the girl herself. Sheila: (bitterly) For letting father and me have her chucked out of her jobs!	"But I accept no blame for it at all" Mrs Birling firmly believes that the,
Mrs Birling: Secondly, I blame the young man who was the father of the child she was going to have. If, as she said, he didn't belong to her class, and was some drunken young idler, then that's all the more reason why he shouldn't escape. He should be made an example of. If the girl's death is due to anybody, then it's due to him.	"drunken young idler" shouldn't escape and that he should be made an example of and that, "If the girl's death is due to anybody, then it's due to him."
Inspector: And if her story id true – that he was stealing money- Mrs Birling: (rather agitated now) There's no point in assuming that- Inspector: But suppose we do, what then?	Mrs Birling is levelling a tirade of abuse at the young man who is responsible, and the audience wished that she was more perceptive. She goes on to say that,
Mrs Birling: Then he'd be entirely responsible – because the girl wouldn't have come to us, and have been refused assistance, if it hadn't been for him- Inspector: So he's the chief culprit anyhow.	"Then he'd be entirely responsible -" And the Inspector probes further into asking her if the young man is, "the chief culprit anyhow"

Mrs Birling: Certainly. And he ought to be dealt with very severely-

Sheila: (*with sudden alarm*) Mother – stop – stop!

Birling: Be quiet, Sheila!
Sheila: But don't you see-

Mrs Birling: (*severely*) You're behaving like an hysterical child tonight.

// Sheila *begins crying quietly.* Mrs Birling *turns to the* Inspector. //

And if you'd take some steps to find this young man and then make sure that he's compelled to confess in public his responsibility – instead of staying here asking quite unnecessary questions – then you really would be doing your duty.

Inspector: (*grimly*) Don't worry Mrs Birling. I shall do my duty. (*He looks at his watch.*)
Mrs Birling: (*triumphantly*) I'm glad to hear it.

Inspector: No hushing up, eh? Make an example of the young man, eh? Public confession of responsibility – um?

Mrs Birling: Certainly. I consider it your duty. And now no doubt you'd like to say good night.
Inspector: Not yet. I'm waiting.
Mrs Birling: Waiting for what?
Inspector: To do my duty.

Sheila: (*distressed*) Now, Mother – don't you see?
Mrs Birling: (*understanding now*) But surely .... I mean ... it's ridiculous . . .

// *she stops and exchanges a frightened glance with her husband.* //

And she vehemently states that,

"Certainly. And he ought to be dealt with very severely-"

Sheila, upon hearing this becomes horrified and quite alarmed, and she rebukes her mother.

"Mother – stop – Stop!"

We see Sheila's desperation to stop her mother's stupidity by Priestley's use of effective punctuation. Mrs Birling accuses Sheila of,

"You're behaving like a hysterical child"

and she shuns Sheila's cries for her to stop and she continues with her tirade of abuse of the young man.

"And if you'd take some steps to find this young man and then make sure that he's compelled to confess in public his responsibility -"

The Inspector seems to be enjoying the way Mrs Birling is 'tightening the noose around her neck' and he triumphantly plays along because he knows who the father of Eva Smith's baby is. Once again Priestley creates some nail-biting tension, and the audience is eager to see Mrs Birling's reaction when she learns that Eric is the father of Eva Smith's child.

"No hushing up, eh? Make an example of the young man, eh? Public confession of responsibility – um?"

The Inspector tells Mrs Birling that he is waiting to do his duty and that he is still waiting. Sheila is now very distressed, and she tells her mother,

"Now Mother – Don't you see?"

Now Mrs Birling knows that Eric is the father, and she stops and exchange a frightened glance with her husband.

TEXT ACT 2 part 9	EXPLANATION
<u>Birling</u>: (*terrified now*) Look Inspector, you're not trying to tell us that – that my boy – is mixed up in this - ? <u>Inspector</u>: (*sternly*) If he is, then we know what to do, don't we? Mrs Birling has just told us. <u>Birling</u>: (*thunderstruck*) My God! But – look here <u>Mrs Birling</u>: (*agitated*) I don't believe it. I won't believe it . . . <u>Sheila</u>: Mother – I begged you and begged you to stop- // *Inspector holds up a hand. We hear the front door. They wait, looking towards door. Eric enters, looking extremely pale and distressed. He meets their inquiring stares.* Curtain falls quickly. // **END OF PART 9** **END OF ACT TWO**	Even Mr Birling becomes terrified and asks, "you're not trying to tell us that – my boy – is mixed up in this - ?" The hyphens and the fragmented speech here suggesting Mr Birling's shock and his fear. The Inspector confirms that Eric is the father and Mr Birling is thunderstruck, "My God! But – look here" Mrs Birling is agitated, and Sheila expresses her disgust, "I don't believe it. I won't believe it . . . " was Mrs Birling's denial as usual. [ERIC ENTERS AND THE CURTAIN FALLS]

[ERIC ENTERS]

The tension in Act 3 is palpable. Eric is standing and the others are staring at him. Right now, I wouldn't want to be in his shoes. He must be feeling mortified.

>"You know, don't you."

Mrs Birling is distressed and quite delusional because she denies that Eric is capable of this.

>"There must be some mistake."

Sheila tells him that their mother has been blaming everything on the young man who got this girl into trouble. Eric is bitter and is disappointed with his mother.

>"You haven't made it any easier for me, have you, Mother?"

Mrs Birling is apologetic and still in denial,

>"you don't get drunk".

Eric asks for a drink which Mr Birling refuses but at the Inspector's request Mr Birling relents and Eric has a drink. He details his relationship with Eva Smith. He met her at the Palace Bar and he was drunk when he got her pregnant. He tells the Inspector that he stole fifty pounds from his father's office and gave it to Eva Smith. Mr Birling was incensed when he heard this. Eric learns of his mother's involvement and he accuses his mother of killing Eva Smith and her own grandchild. Mr Birling asks Eric why he didn't come to him for help when he got himself into this mess. Eric says that he's not the kind of father one can go to for help. This indicates the distance between father and son. They seem very detached. This scene is very dramatic and explosive because Eric shouts at his mother, and Mr Birling also shouts at Eric and almost gets physical and then the Inspector promptly intervenes and stops their bickering. Towards the end of the play, the Inspector sends his poignant messages about responsibility, social injustices, and class prejudices home to the Birlings, as Priestley intended him to do.

He targets their conscience and outlays in detail each of their roles in the demise of Eva Smith. Although, she is dead, he says that,

>"there are millions and millions of Eva Smiths and John Smiths still left with us."

He warns them that we all have a responsibility and a moral duty to care for each other and if we don't learn that lesson then man,

>"will be taught it in fire and anguish."

referring to the end of the world and man answering to God or face hell's fire.

He delivers his final speech and leaves. Sheila is wise and she is suspicious whether the Inspector was really a policeman. Mr Birling accuses Eric and Sheila of telling the Inspector their secrets, hence being fooled by him.

Gerald returns and tells them that the Inspector is a fake because his friend – a police sergeant – told him that there was no Inspector Goole in the force. Mr Birling is excited, and he immediately telephones his friend, Colonel Roberts. Then the battle of the generations ensues because Sheila and Eric are shocked at their parent's behaviour. Both accuse them of pretending like nothing has happened. They insist that even if the Inspector is a 'fake', they still participated in the actions that led to Eva Smith's death. Eric makes constant reference to the girl being dead and that they all contributed to killing her.

Gerald tries to unravel this mystery and using the photographs as a lead, he insists that they were not responsible for Eva Smith's death. The photographs, he says could have been of different girls. He telephones the infirmary and enquires about the death by poisoning of one of their employees. He is relieved to learn that there was no such death. Gerald attempts to give Sheila back the engagement ring, but she refused it.

The telephone rings sharply and a policeman tells Mr Birling that a girl has died after swallowing some disinfectant and that an Inspector is on his way to question them. The end of the play is riveting as they stare guiltily and shocked.
Another Inspector is coming to question them. The older generation are very content, and Mr Birling says,
> "you'll have a good laugh over it yet."
Sheila is outraged at her parents' coldness,
> "you are ready to go on in the same old way."
Priestley is trying to warn the Birlings that as long as they refuse to take responsibility, the Inspector will always come back to haunt them and point out the error of their ways because at the end we see another police Inspector coming to question them.

[THE FAMILY STARE GUILTILY AND DUMBFOUNDED]

START OF PART 10

//Exactly as at the end of Act Two. Eric is standing just inside the room and the others are staring at him. //

Eric: You know, don't you?
Inspector: (*as before*) Yes, we know.

// Eric shuts the door and comes farther in. //

Mrs Birling: (*distressed*) Eric, I can't believe it. There must be some mistake. You don't know what we've been saying.
  Sheila: It's a good job for him he doesn't, isn't it?
Eric: Why?
Sheila: Because mother's been busy blaming everything on the young man who got this girl into trouble, and saying he shouldn't escape and should be made an example of-
  Birling: That's enough, Sheila.

Eric: (*bitterly*) You haven't made it any easier for me, have you, Mother?

Mrs Birling: But I didn't know it was you – I never dreamt. Besides, you're not the type – you don't get drunk-

  Sheila: Of course, he does. I told you he did.

Eric: You told her. Why, you little sneak!

  Sheila: No, that's not fair, Eric. I could have told her months ago, but of course I didn't. I only told her tonight because I knew everything was coming out – it was simply bound to come out tonight – so I thought she might as well know in advance. Don't forget – I've already been through it.
  Mrs Birling: Sheila, I simply don't understand your attitude.

[ERIC AND THE INSPECTOR]

INSPECTOR with ERIC viewing PHOTOGRAPH

It will be important to compare the change in attitude of the Birlings in Act 3 to that of Act 1 and Act 2. In Act 3 they are not so bold and confident as they used to be. Priestley gives us a visual picture of everyone staring at Eric who is extremely pale and distressed. Once again, we see the family dissention. Eric is bitter towards Mrs Birling,

"You haven't made it any easier for me, have you, Mother?"

Mrs Birling is still in denial about Eric's drinking. She tells Eric,

"you are not the type – you don't get drunk"

Eric accuses Sheila of exposing his drinking secrets to his mother and he is furious with her,

"You told her. Why, you little sneak!"

Sheila defends her action, and we once again see her sense of perception because she knew that everyone's secrets are going to be exposed by the Inspector.

"I knew everything was coming out"

There is also a sense of detachment between Eric and Mrs Birling because he couldn't communicate his problems to his mother. Mrs Birling is furious with Sheila, and she accuses her of being disloyal.

"Sheila, I simply don't understand your attitude"

Birling: Neither do I. If you'd had any sense of loyalty-

Inspector: (*cutting in, smoothly*) Just a minute, Mr Birling. There be plenty of time, when I've gone, for you all to adjust your family relationships. But now I must hear what your son has to tell me. (*sternly, to the three of them.*) And I'll be obliged if you'll let us get on without any further interruptions. (*turning to* Eric.) Now then.

Eric: (*miserably*) Could I have a drink first?

Birling: (*explosively*) No.

Inspector: (*firmly*) Yes. (*As Birling looks like interrupting explosively*.) I know – he's your son and this is your house – but look at him. He needs a drink now just to see him through.

Birling: (*To* Eric) All right. Go on.

// *Eric goes for a whisky. His whole manner of handling the decanter and then the drink shows his familiarity with quick heavy drinking. The others watch him narrowly.* //

(*bitterly*) I understand a lot of things now I didn't understand before.

Inspector: Don't start on that. I want to get on. (*To* Eric.) When did you first meet this girl?

Eric: One night last November.

Inspector: where did you meet her?

Eric: In the Palace Bar. I'd been there an hour or so with two or three chaps. I was a bit squiffy.

Inspector: What happened then?

Eric: I began talking to her, and stood her a few drinks. I was rather far gone by the time we had to go.

Inspector: Was she drunk too?

Eric: She told me afterwards that she was a bit, chiefly because she'd not had much to eat that day.

Inspector: Why had she gone there-?

Eric: She wasn't the usual sort. But – well, I suppose she didn't know what to do. There was some woman who wanted to help her go there. I never quite understood about that.

Mr Birling vents out his frustration with Sheila and agrees with Mrs Birling that she is disloyal for siding with the Inspector.

It's surprising how Mr Birling gives in to the Inspector's demands when the Inspector gives Eric permission to have a drink. Mr Birling says,

"All right, Go on"

If we look at the stage directions, Priestley tells us that at this point the Birlings are 'miserable', 'bitter', 'explosive' and 'distressed'. One can connote that the Inspector has successfully managed to bring down the Birlings a peg or two from their high pedestal. He even caused them to quarrel and be at loggerheads with each other. Eric tells the Inspector of his meeting with Eva Smith.

PALACE BAR

Inspector: You went with her to her lodgings that night?

Eric: Yes, I insisted – it seems. I'm not very clear about it, but afterwards she told me she didn't want me to go in but that – well, I was in that state when a chap easily turns nasty – and I threatened to make a row.

Inspector: So she let you in?

Eric: Yes. And that's when it happened. And I didn't even remember – that's the hellish thing. Oh – my God! - how stupid it all is!

Mrs Birling: (*with a cry*) Oh – Eric – how could you?

Birling: (*sharply*) Sheila, take your mother along to the drawing-room--

Sheila: (*protesting*) But – I want to –

Birling: (*very sharply*) You heard what I said. (*Gentler*.) Go on, Sybil.

// He goes to open the door while Sheila takes her mother out. Then he closes it and comes in. //

Inspector: When did you meet her again?

Eric: About a fortnight afterwards.

Inspector: By appointment?

Eric: No. And I couldn't remember her name or where she lived. It was all very vague.

But I happened to see her again in the Palace bar.

Inspector: More drinks?

Eric: Yes, though that time I wasn't so bad.

Inspector: But you took her home again?

Eric: Yes. And this time we talked a bit. She told me something about herself and I talked too. Told her my name and what I did.

Inspector: And you made love again?

Eric: Yes. I wasn't in love with her or anything – but I liked her – she was pretty and a good sport--

Birling: (*harshly*) So you had to go to bed with her?

Eric: Well, I'm old enough to be married, aren't I, and I'm not married, and I hate these fat old tarts round the town – the ones I see some of your respectable friends with--

MRS BIRLING – SHEILA – INSPECTOR - ERIC

[MRS BIRLING AND SHEILA EXIT THE ROOM]

ERIC – INSPECTOR GOOLE – ARTHUR

Birling: (*angrily*) I don't want any of that talk from you-
Inspector: (*very sharply*) I don't want any of it from either of you. Settle it afterwards. (*To* Eric.) did you arrange to see each other after that?

Eric: Yes. And the next time – or the time after that – she told me she thought she was going to have a baby. She wasn't quite sure. And then she was.
Inspector: And of course, she was very worried about it?

Eric: Yes, and so was I. I was in a hell of a state about it.

Inspector: Did she suggest that you ought to marry her?

Eric: No. she didn't want me to marry her. Said I didn't love her – and all that. In a way, she treated me – as if I were a kid. Though I was nearly as old as she was.

Inspector: So what did you propose to do?
Eric: Well, she hadn't a job – and didn't feel like trying again for one – and she'd no money left – so I insisted on giving her enough money to keep her going – until she refused to take any more--
Inspector: How much did you give her altogether?
Eric: I suppose – about fifty pounds all told.

Birling: Fifty pounds – on top of drinking and going around the town! Where did you get fifty pounds from?
// *As Eric does not reply.* //

Inspector: That's my question too.
Eric: (*miserably*) I got it – from the office--

Birling: My office?

Eric: Yes.

Inspector: You mean – you stole the money?

Mr Birling became very harsh and angry at Eric when he heard the details.

"I don't want any of that talk from you."

But the Inspector became very assertive and retorted,

"I don't want any of it from either of you. Settle it afterwards."

The Inspector probes Eric about his affair with Eva Smith. Eric tells the Inspector that Eva Smith told him that she was pregnant.
He was very worried,

"I was in a hell of a state"

Eric talked about Eva Smith's refusal to marry him because he did not love her.

"No, she didn't want me to marry her. Said I didn't love her"

Once again, we see friction in the family, now between Eric and his father. Mr Birling is furious when he hears that Eric gave Eva Smith fifty pounds.

"Fifty pounds – on top of drinking and going around the town!"

And astounded when Eric admits he took the fifty pounds from Mr Birling's office

"My office?"

The Inspector then clarifies the issue,

"You mean – you stole the money?"

Eric: Not really.

Birling: (*angrily*) What do you mean – not really?

// Eric does not reply because now Mrs Birling and Sheila come back. //

Sheila: This isn't my fault.

Mrs Birling: (*To* Birling) I'm sorry, Arthur, but I simply couldn't stay in there. I had to know what's happening.

Birling: (*savagely*) Well, I can tell you what's happening. He's admitted he was responsible for the girl's condition, and now he's telling us he supplied her with money he stole from the office.

Mrs Birling: (*shocked*) Eric! You stole money?

Eric: No, not really. I intended to pay it back.

Birling: We've heard that story before. How could you have paid it back?

Eric: I'd have managed somehow. I had to have some money-

Birling: I don't understand how you could take as much as that out of the office without somebody knowing.

Eric: There were some small accounts to collect, and I asked for cash--

Birling: Gave the firm's receipt and then kept the money, eh?

Eric: Yes.

Birling: You must give me a list of those accounts. I've got to cover this up as soon as I can. You damned fool – why didn't you come to me when you found yourself in this mess?

Eric: Because you're not the kind of father a chap could go to when he's in trouble – that's why.

Birling: (*angrily*) Don't talk to me like that. Your trouble is – you've been spoilt--

---

Eric then dismisses the Inspector's claim by saying,

"Not really"

Mr Birling, realising the seriousness of Eric's dishonest behaviour, and retorts,

"What do you mean – not really?"

[ENTER MRS BIRLING AND SHEILA]

Mrs Birling learns that he stole the money and she's shocked,

"Eric! You stole money?"

As I mentioned earlier that there was a strained and distant relationship between Eric and Mr Birling. We tend to empathise with Eric here when Mr Birling says,

"- why didn't you come to me when you found yourself I this mess."

Eric confirms this detachment when he tells his father,

"Because you're not the kind of father a chap could go to when he's in trouble"

ERIC with EVA SMITH alias DAISY RENTON

Inspector: (*cutting in*) And my trouble is – that I haven't much time. You'll be able to divide the responsibility between you when I've gone. (*To* Eric.) Just one last question, that's all. The girl discovered that this money you were giving her was stolen, didn't she?

Eric: (*miserably*) Yes. That was the worst of all. She wouldn't take any more, and she didn't want to see me again. (*sudden startled tone*.) Here, but how did you know that? Did she tell you?

Inspector: No. she told me nothing. I never spoke to her.

Sheila: She told mother.

Mrs Birling: (*alarmed*) Sheila!

Sheila: Well, he has to know.

Eric: (*to* Mrs Birling) She told you? Did she come here – but then she couldn't have done, she didn't even know I lived here. What happened?

// Mrs Birling, *distressed, shakes her head bout does not reply.* //

Come on, don't just look like that. Tell me – tell me – what happened?

Inspector: (*with calm authority*) I'll tell you. She went to your mother's committee for help, after she'd done with you. Your mother refused that help.

Eric: (*nearly at breaking point*) Then – you killed her. She came to you to protect me – and you turned her away – yes, and you killed her – and the child she'd have had too – my child – your own grandchild – you killed them both – damn you, damn you–

Mrs Birling: (*very distressed now*) No – Eric – please – I didn't know – I didn't understand-

Eric: (*almost threatening her*) You don't understand anything. You never did. You never even tried – you -

Sheila: (*frightened*) Eric, don't – don't-

Birling: (*furious, intervening*) Why, you hysterical young fool – get back – or I'll-

Finally, we see a distressed Mrs Birling caught in a trap. Eric hears about how Eva Smith went to his mother for help and she refused to help her. He is at breaking point and tells his mother,

"Then – you killed her"
"– my child–
"– your own grandchild –"
"– you killed them both –"
"– damn you, damn you–"

Eric is very passionate here and Mrs Birling is distressed now and pleads with him to understand,

"No – Eric – please – I didn't know."

The use of the repeated hyphens suggest that Mrs Birling is full of emotions and is struggling to complete her sentence fluidly.

Mr Birling intervenes furiously,

"Why, you hysterical young fool – get back – or I'll-"

They seem to be almost coming to blows. The situation is very tense and dramatic. Once again, the Inspector managed to create a family feud.

Inspector: (*taking charge, masterfully*) Stop!

// *They are suddenly quiet, staring at him.* //

And be quiet for a moment and listen to me. I don't need to know any more. Neither do you. This girl killed herself – and died a horrible death. But each of you helped to kill her. Remember that. Never forget it. (*He looks from one to the other of them carefully.*) But then I don't think you ever will. Remember what you did, Mrs Birling. You turned her away when she most needed help. You refused her even the pitiable little bit of organized charity you had in your power to grant her. Remember what you did-

Eric: (*unhappily*) My God – I'm not likely to forget.
Inspector: Just used her for the end of a stupid drunken evening, as if she was an animal, a thing, not a person. No, you won't forget. (*He looks at Sheila.*)
Sheila: (*bitterly*) I know. I had her turned out of a job. I started it.

Inspector: You helped – but you didn't start it. (*rather savagely, to Birling.*) You started it. She wanted twenty-five shillings a week instead of twenty-two and sixpence. You made her pay a heavy price for that. And now she'll make you pay a heavier price still.
Birling: (*unhappily*) Look, Inspector – I'd give thousands – yes, thousands-

Inspector: You're offering the money at the wrong time. Mr Birling. (*He makes a move as if concluding the session, possibly shutting up notebook, etc. Then surveys them sardonically.*) No, I don't think any of you will forget. Nor that young man, Croft, though he at least had some affection for her and made her happy for a time. Well, Eva Smith's gone. You can't do her any more harm. And you can't do her any good now, either. You can't even say "I'm sorry, Eva Smith."

Sheila: (*who is crying quietly*) That's the worst of it.

The Inspector masterfully takes charge,

"Stop!"

And they are suddenly quiet, staring at him. They are all under the control of the Inspector and he tells them,

"The girl killed herself-"
"and died a horrible death."
"But each of you helped to kill her."
"Remember that?"
"Never forget it."

The Inspector tries to target their conscience and prick at it individually. He personally tells each of them about the role they played in Eva Smith's death.

The Inspector rejects Mr Birling's offer of thousand pounds,

"You're offering the money at the wrong time"

And sarcastically comments to the Birlings and Gerald,

"Well, Eva Smith's gone."
"You can't do her any more harm."
"And you can't do her any good now, either."

While Sheila is crying quietly, the Inspector concludes by reminding them that,

Inspector: But just remember this. One Eva Smith has gone – but there are millions and millions and millions of Eva Smiths and John Smiths still left with us, with their lives, their hopes and fears, their suffering and chance of happiness, all intertwined with our lives, and what we think and say and do. We don't live alone. We are members of one body. We are responsible for each other. And I tell you that the time will soon come when, if men will not learn that lesson, then they will be taught it in fire and blood and anguish. Good night.

// He walks straight out, leaving them staring, subdued and wondering. Sheila is still quietly crying. Mrs Birling has collapsed into a chair. Eric is brooding desperately. Birling, the only active one, hears the front door slam, moves hesitatingly towards the door, stops, looks gloomily at the other three, then pours himself out a drink, which he hastily swallows. //

END OF PART 10

"One Eva Smith has gone – But there are millions and millions of Eva Smiths and John Smiths still left with us."

He is making reference to the poor socialist class with their hopes and fears and their sufferings all intertwined with our lives, and what we think, and say, and do. The Inspector's concluding speech is very very powerful because he warns the Birlings that,

"We don't live alone."
"We are responsible for each other."

He is trying to instil in them, as Priestley wanted him to do, a sense of social responsibility and help the less fortunate in Society. The 'One body' here can be a biblical reference to the body of Christ who sacrificed himself by dying on the cross to save the world. The Inspector concludes by using a very powerful biblical imagery,

"If men will not learn that lesson,
then they will be taught it
in fire and blood and anguish"

START OF PART 11

Birling: (*angrily to Eric*) You're the one I blame for this.

Eric: I'll bet I am.

Birling: (*angrily*) Yes, and you don't realize yet all you've done. Most of this is bound to come out. There'll be a public scandal.

Eric: Well, I don't care now.

Birling: You! You don't seem to care about anything. But I care. I was almost certain for a knighthood in the next Honours List-

// Eric laughs rather hysterically, pointing at him. /

Eric: (*laughing*) Oh – for God's sake! What does it matter now weather they give you a knighthood or not?

Birling: (*sternly*) It doesn't matter to you. Apparently, nothing matters to you. But it may interest you to know that until every penny of that money you stole is repaid, you'll work for nothing. And there's going to be no more of this drinking round the town – and picking up women in the Palace bar-

Mrs Birling: (*coming to life*) I should think not. Eric, I'm absolutely ashamed of you.

Eric: Well, I don't blame you. But don't forget I'm ashamed of you as well – yes both of you.

Birling: (*angrily*) Drop that. There's every excuse for what both your mother and I did – it turned out unfortunately, that's all--

Sheila: (*scornfully*) That's all.

Birling: Well, what have you to say?

Sheila: I don't know where to begin.

Birling: Then don't begin. Nobody wants you to.

Mr Birling very conveniently blames Eric for this mess. Now he is not concerned about Eric's mental state but about social status. He angrily retorts,

"You're the one I blame for this"

And he is even more worried because he says that,

"There'll be a public scandal"

Mr Birling's selfish, social climbing, and greed is evident here because his family is in agony and he puts his needs first,

"I was almost certain for a knighthood in the next honours list"

There seems to be a battle between the older and new generation here because Eric tells his parents,

"I'm ashamed of you as well – yes both of you"

ARTHUR – ERIC - SYBIL

Sheila: I behaved badly too. I know I did I'm ashamed of it. But now you're beginning all over again to pretend that nothing much has happened-

Birling: Nothing much has happened! Haven't I already said there'll be a public scandal – unless we're lucky – and who here will suffer from that more than I will?

Sheila: But that's not what I'm talking about. I don't care about that. The point is, you don't seem to have learnt anything.

Birling: Don't I? Well, you're quite wrong there. I've learnt plenty tonight. And you don't want me to tell you what I've learnt, I hope. When I look back on tonight – when I think of what I was feeling when the five of us sat down to dinner at that table-

Eric: (*cutting in*) Yes, and do you remember what you said to Gerald and me after dinner, when you were feeling so pleased with yourself? You told us that a man has to make his own way, look after himself and mind his own business, and that we weren't to take any notice of these cranks who tell us that everybody has to look after everybody else, as if we were all mixed up together. Do you remember? Yes – and then one of those cranks walked in – the Inspector. (*laughs bitterly.*) I didn't notice you told him that it's every man for himself.

Sheila: (*sharply attentive*) Is that when the Inspector came, just after father had said that?
Eric: Yes. What of it?
Mrs Birling: Now what's the matter, Sheila?
Sheila: (*slowly*) It's queer – very queer - (*she looks at them reflectively*.)
Mrs Birling: (*with some excitement*) I know what you're going to say. Because I've been wondering myself.

Sheila acknowledges that she did wrong, but she is shocked about her parent's causal attitude to the whole situation,

"to pretend that nothing much has happened"

Both Sheila and Eric attack their parent's insensitivity and Priestley hopes that the new generation will make a change and take responsibility in Society and make it better. Sheila seems to be at her wits-end with her parent's attitude because by now she has proven to be fully developed and matured as compared to the beginning of the play. She is bold enough to confront her parents,

"you don't seem to have learnt anything"

Eric levels a scathing attack on his father, he reminds him of his earlier grand speech,

"a man has to make his own way, look after himself - And mind his own business"

Eric's bitterness and fury spills over as he reminds his father of the selfish lesson, he has taught them earlier. He also challenges his father and he wanted to know why he didn't tell the Inspector that

"it's every man for himself"

Implying that he was scared of the Inspector.

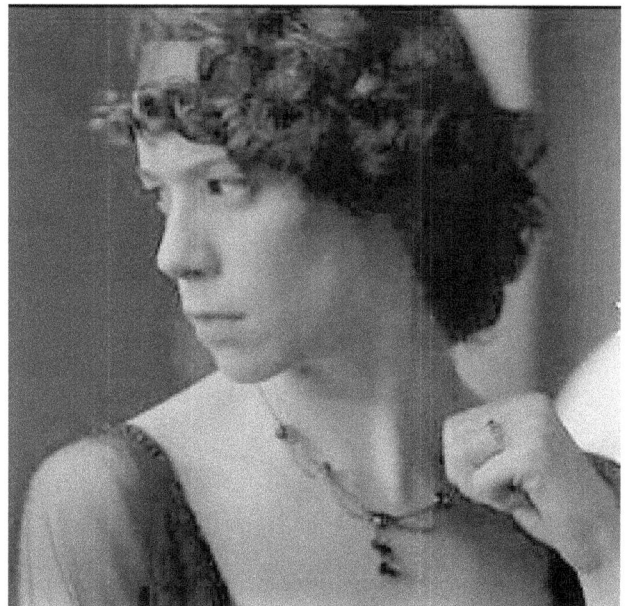

SHEILA relies It's queer – very queer

Sheila: It doesn't much matter now, of course – but was he really a police inspector?

Birling: Well, if he wasn't, it matters a devil of a lot. Makes all the difference.

Sheila: No, it doesn't.

Birling: Don't talk rubbish. Of course, it does.

Sheila: Well, it doesn't to me. And it oughtn't to you, either.

Mrs Birling: Don't be childish, Sheila.

Sheila: (*flaring up*) I'm not being. If you want to know, it's you two who are being childish – trying not to face the facts.

Birling: I won't have that sort of talk. Any more of that and you leave this room.

Eric: That'll be terrible for her, won't it?

Sheila: I'm going anyhow in a minute or two. But don't you see, if all that's come out tonight is true, then it doesn't much matter who it was who made us confess. And it was true, wasn't it? You turned the girl out of one job, and I had her turned out of another. Gerald kept her – at a time when he was supposed to be too busy to see me. Eric – well, we know what Eric did. And mother hardened her heart and gave her the final push that finished her. That's what's important – and not whether a man is a police inspector or not.

Eric: He was our police inspector all right.

Sheila: That's what I mean, Eric. But if it's any comfort to you – and it wasn't to me – I have an idea – and I had it all alone vaguely – that there was something curious about him. He never seemed like an ordinary police inspector-

Birling: (*rather excited*) you're right. I felt it too. (*To* Mrs Birling.) Didn't you?

Mrs Birling: Well, I must say his manner was quite extraordinary; so – so rude – and assertive -

Sheila once again shows us a renewed level of maturity. She unravels the fact that he wasn't a real police officer. She was the only one to have her suspicions.   Sheila becomes furious with her mother, and flares up when her mother accuses her of being childish, and she retorts,

"It's you two who are being childish
- trying not to face the facts"

We can trace Sheila's maturity and development from a naïve young girl to that of mature, strong woman at the end of the play. Priestley created this very admirable character to reflect his passion that the younger generation will become the ambassadors of social change in rigid, avaricious Edwardian Society. Sheila attacks her mother for her harsh treatment of Eva Smith,

"And mother hardened her heart and gave her the final push and that finished her"

Mr Birling is very irate with Sheila, and he asks her to leave. But before she does, she tries to point out the error of her parent's ways. She emphases the fact that the truth about what they did to Eva Smith was revealed irrespective of who pointed it out.

The younger generation both Sheila and Eric join forces in attempting to change their parent's selfish ways.

Birling: Then look at the way he talked to me. Telling me to shut up – and so on. He must have known I was an ex-Lord Mayor and a magistrate and so forth. Besides – the way he talked – you remember. I mean, they don't talk like that. I've had dealings with dozens of them.

Sheila: All right. But it doesn't make any real difference, y'know.
Mrs Birling: Of course, it does.

Eric: No, Sheila's right. It doesn't.

Birling: (*angrily*) That's comic, that is, coming from you. You're the one it makes most difference to. You've confessed to theft, and now he knows all about it, and he can bring it out at the inquest, and then if necessary, carry it to court. He can't do anything to your mother and Sheila and me – except perhaps make us look a bit ashamed of ourselves in public – but as for you, he can ruin you. You know.

Sheila: (*slowly*) We hardly ever told him anything he didn't know. Did you notice that?

Birling: That's nothing. He had a bit of information, left by the girl, and made a few smart guesses – but the fact remains that if we hadn't talked so much, he'd have had little to go on. (*looks angrily at them*.) And really, when I come to think of it, why you all had to go letting everything come out like that, beats me.
Sheila: It's all right talking like that now. But he made us confess.
Mrs Birling: He certainly didn't make me confess – as you call it. I told him quite plainly that I thought I had done no more than my duty.
Sheila: Oh – Mother!
Birling: The fact is, you allowed yourselves to be bluffed. Yes – bluffed.
Mrs Birling: (*protesting*) Now really – Arthur.

When Mr Birling complains about the Inspector's rude mannerisms towards him, Sheila says,

"But it doesn't make any real difference"

because they were guilty of contributing to Eva Smith's death.

Eric boldly steps in and agrees with Sheila.

"No, Sheila's right. It doesn't."

Mr Birling attacks Eric for his indiscretion for getting Eva Smith pregnant. He angrily tells Eric that he can be accused of theft and warns Eric that the Inspector can ruin him. Sheila's sense of perception and foresight once again surfaces. She was aware that the Inspector knew everything about them.

"We hardly ever told him anything he didn't know. Did you notice that?"

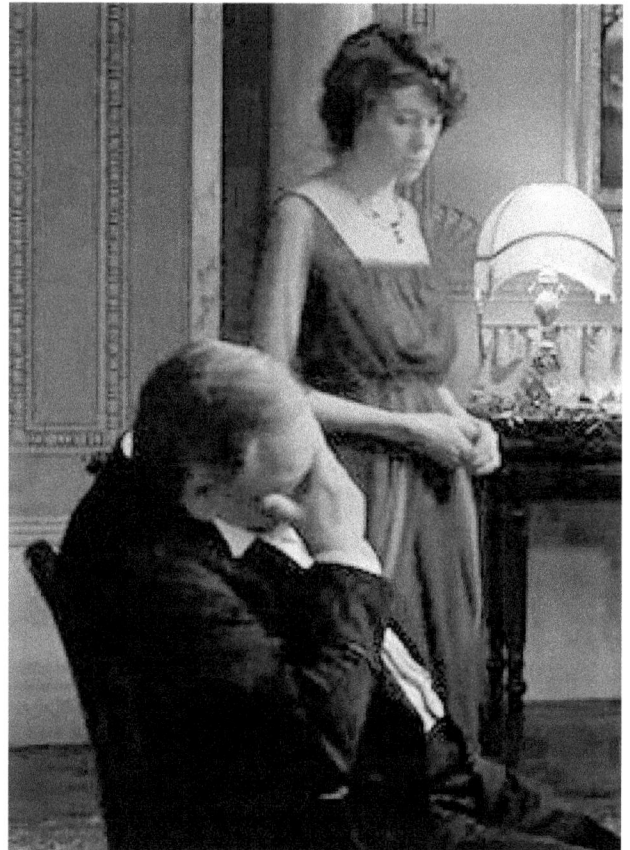

ARTHUR despondent next to SHEILA

Birling: No, not you, my dear. But these two. That fellow obviously didn't like us. He was prejudiced from the start. Probably a socialist or some sort of crank – he talked like one. And then, instead of standing up to him, you let him bluff you into talking about your private affairs. You ought to have stood up to him.

Eric: (*sulkily*) Well, I didn't notice you standing up to him.

Birling: No, because by that time you'd admitted you'd been taking money. What chance had I after that? I was a fool not to have insisted upon seeing him alone.

Eric: That wouldn't have worked.

Sheila: Of course it wouldn't.

Mrs Birling: Really, from the way you children talk, you might be wanting to help him instead of us. Now just be quiet so that your father can decide what we ought to do. (*Looks expectantly at* Birling.)

Birling: (*dubiously*) Yes – well. We'll have to do something – and get to work quickly too.

// As he hesitates there is a ring at the front door. They look at each other in alarm. //

Now who's this? Had I better go?

Mrs Birling: No. Edna'll go. I asked her to wait up to make us some tea.

Sheila: It might be Gerald coming back.

Birling: (*relieved*) Yes, of course. I'd forgotten about him.

END OF PART 11

It's obvious and Sheila is right that her parents – didn't learn anything from this experience because Mr Birling is absolutely shocking,

"Probably a Socialist or some sort of crank."

He is still attacking the Socialist. Furthermore, he is blaming Eric and Sheila for talking about their private affairs yet he himself was afraid of the Inspector. He even agreed for Eric to have a drink at the Inspector's request when he had actually turned him down.

He tells them that,

"You ought to have stood up to him."

But Eric rightfully pointed out that,

"I didn't notice you standing up to him."

Once again, the symbolism of the bell rings clear here and creates a lot of suspense. Another entrance helps to move the plot along. The audience becomes curious as to who it is.

START OF PART 12

// Edna appears. //

Edna: It's Mr Croft.

// Gerald appears, and Edna withdraws. //

Gerald: I hope you don't mind my coming back?

Mrs Birling: No, of course not, Gerald.

Gerald: I had a special reason for coming. When did that Inspector go?

Sheila: Only a few minutes ago. He put us all through it -

Mrs Birling: (*warningly*) Sheila!

Sheila: Gerald might as well know.

Birling: (*hastily*) Now – now – we needn't bother him with all that stuff.

Sheila: All right. (*To* Gerald.) But we're all in it – up to the neck. It got worse after you left.

Gerald: How did he behave?

Sheila: He was – frightening.

Birling: If you ask me, he behaved in a very peculiar and suspicious manner.

Mrs Birling: The rude way he spoke to Mr Birling and me – it was quite extraordinary!

Gerald: Hm -hm!

//they all look inquiringly at Gerald. //

Birling: (*excitedly*) You know something. What is it?

Gerald: (*slowly*) That man wasn't a police officer.

Birling: (*astounded*) What?

Mrs Birling: Are you certain?

Gerald: I'm almost certain. That's what I came back to tell you.

Birling: (*excitedly*) Good lad! You asked about him, eh?

Gerald: Yes. I met a police sergeant I know down the road. I asked him about this Inspector Goole and described the chap carefully to him. He swore there wasn't any Inspector Goole or anybody like him on the force here.

Birling: You didn't tell him-

[GERALD ENTERS]

GERALD CROFT

Gerald tells the Birlings that the Inspector wasn't a real police officer. Mr Birling phones his friend the police Chief Colonel Roberts and asks him if Inspector Goole has joined his Staff and was relieved to discover that no such Inspector exists. Note the significance of the name 'Goole' which sounds mysterious or ghostly just like the Inspector.

Mr Birling is excited, and he is keen that Gerald didn't tell the police sergeant about the family's secret. Once again Mr Birling is trying to protect his reputation.

"You didn't tell him-"

Gerald's lying character once again surfaces because he lies to the sergeant that he was having an argument with somebody.

Gerald: (*cutting in*) No, no. passed it off by saying I'd been having an argument with somebody. But the point is – this sergeant was dead certain they hadn't any inspector at all like the chap who came here.

Birling: (*excitedly*) By jingo! A fake!

Mrs Birling: (*triumphantly*) Didn't I tell you? Didn't I say I couldn't imagine a real police inspector talking like that to us?

Gerald: Well, you were right. There isn't any such inspector. We've been had.

Birling: (*beginning to move*) I'm going to make certain of this.

Mrs Birling: What are you going to do?

Birling: Ring up the chief constable – Colonel Roberts.

Mrs Birling: Careful what you say, dear.

Birling: (*now at telephone*) Of course. (*At telephone.*) Brumley eight seven five two. (*To others as he waits.*) I was going to do this anyhow. I've had my suspicions all along. (*At telephone.*) Colonel Roberts, please. Mr Arthur Birling here . . . oh, Roberts – Birling here. Sorry to ring you up so late, but can you tell me if an Inspector Goole has joined your staff lately. . . Goole. G -O-O-L-E . . . a new man . . . tall , clean-shaven. (*Here he can describe the appearance of the actor playing the Inspector.*) I see . . . yes . . . well, that settles it. . . . No, just a little argument we were having here. . . . Good night. (*He puts down the telephone and looks at the others.*) There's no Inspector Goole on the police. That man definitely wasn't a police inspector at all. As Gerald says – we've been had.

END OF PART 12

By Birling is suddenly very excited and vibrant because he can now go back to his old way of life. Note how quickly he forgot the death of his employee which he was responsible for.

"By jingo! A fake!"

ARTHUR BIRLING on the phone to COLONEL ROBERTS

Mrs Birling is also triumphant like her husband
And she too forgot about her role in Eva Smith's death.

Mr Birling goes to ring the chief constable – Colonel Roberts. Mrs Birling too is very careful about their reputation and asks him to be careful what he says.

We have observed the character of the Capitalist class who were supposed to be upstanding members of Society but have no qualms about lying. Here Mr Birling also lies to the Colonel.

"No just a little argument we were having here"

Mr Birling confirms the news that,

"There's no Inspector Goole on the police"

Mr Birling says,

"As Gerald says - we've been had"

meaning that they had been fooled by the Inspector.

START OF PART 13

Mrs Birling: I felt it all the time. He never talked like one. He never even looked like one.

Birling: This makes a difference, y'know. In fact, it makes all the difference.

Gerald: Of course!

Sheila: (*bitterly*) I suppose we're all nice people now.

Birling: If you've nothing more sensible than that to say, Sheila you'd better keep quiet.

Eric: She's right, though.

Birling: (*angrily*) And you'd better keep quiet anyhow. If that had been a police inspector and he'd heard you confess-

Mrs Birling: (*warningly*) Arthur – careful!

Birling: (*hastily*) Yes, yes.

Sheila: You see, Gerald, you haven't to know the rest of our crimes and idiocies.

Gerald: That's all right, I don't want to. (*To* birling.) What do you make of this business now? Was it a hoax?

Birling: Of course. Somebody put that fellow up to coming here and hoaxing us. There are people in this town who dislike me enough to do that. We ought to have seen through it from the first. In the ordinary way, I believe I would have done. But coming like that, bang on top of our little celebration, just when we were all feeling so pleased with ourselves, naturally it took me by surprise.

Mrs Birling: I wish I'd been here when that man first arrived. I'd have asked him a few questions before I allowed him to ask us any.

Sheila: It's all right saying that now.

SYBIL – ARTHUR - SHEILA

Mr & Mrs Birling and Gerald are rather thrilled that the Inspector was a 'fake'. But Sheila is incensed at their attitude, and she bitterly cries out,

"I suppose we're all nice people now."

Another argument between the younger and older generation ensues. Mr and Mrs Birling are trying to hush Eric's secret about Eva Smith, but Sheila wants to let the cat out of the bag and says,

"You see, Gerald, you haven't to know
the rest of our crimes and idiocies"

Mr Birling and Gerald theorize about the Inspector being a hoax and Mr Birling says,

"We ought to have seen through it from the first"

Mr Birling is trying to act brave and regain his status like the way he did when he gave his selfish speech to Eric and Gerald earlier on in the play,

"We are not like bees in a hive"

Mrs Birling is mirroring her husband and is also acting brave but only after the Inspector left.

"I'd have asked him a few questions before I allowed him to ask us any"

Sheila reacts with a very bitter tone to her mother's absurd remark.

"It's all right saying that now"

Mrs Birling: I was the only one of you who didn't give in to him. And now I say we must discuss this business quietly and sensibly and decide if there's anything to be done about it.

Birling: (*with hearty approval*) You're absolutely right, my dear. Already we've discovered one important fact – that that fellow was a fraud and we've been hoaxed – and that may not be the end of it by any means.

Gerald: I'm sure it isn't.
Birling: (*keenly interested*) You are, eh? Good! (*To* Eric, *who is restless.*) Eric, sit down.
Eric: (*sulkily*) I'm all right.

Birling: All right? You're anything but all right. And you needn't stand there – as if – as if –

Eric: As if – what?

Birling: As if you'd nothing to do with us. Just remember your own position, young man. If anybody's up to the neck in this business, you are, so you'd better take some interest in it.

Eric: I do take some interest in it. I take too much, that's my trouble.
Sheila: It's mine too.

Birling: Now listen, you two. If you're still feeling on edge, then the least you can do is to keep quiet. Leave this to us. I'll admit that fellow's antics rattled us a bit. But we've found him out – and all we have to do is to keep our heads. Now it's our turn.

Sheila: Our turn to do – what?
Mrs Birling: (*sharply*) To behave sensibly, Sheila – which is more than you're doing.

Eric: (*bursting out*) What's the use of talking about behaving sensibly. You're beginning to pretend now that nothing's really happened at all. And I can't see it like that. This girl's still dead, isn't she? Nobody's brought her to life, have they?

Mr Birling seem to have got his spunk back and acting important in trying to solve the puzzle.

"that fellow was a fraud and we've been hoaxed"

There is a tense exchange between Eric and Mr Birling. We notice that Eric too has matured because he too stands up to his father's arrogant attitude. Mr Birling is furious with Eric and tells him

"And you needn't stand there - as if – as if -"

In response, Eric challenges his father,

"As if – what?"

Mr Birling shoves all the blame on Eric,

"If anybody's up to the neck in this business, you are"

Mr Birling insists that Eric take some action in solving the problem because Gerald too seems to be fired up and is trying to solve the problem of finding out who the Inspector actually was.

Mr Birling is trying to assume control and asks Sheila and Eric, who share the same views about their parent's bizarre attitude, to be quiet and leave everything to them.
Mr Birling also admits that the Inspector unnerved them a bit.

"I'll admit that fellow's antics rattled us a bit."

Eric is disgusted about his parent's behaviour, he too says,

"you're beginning to pretend now that nothing's really happened at all"

He seems to be echoing Sheila's words. Once again, we see the clashes between the generations. He goes on to point out,

"This girl's still dead, isn't she?"

Sheila: (*eagerly*) That's just what I feel, Eric. And it's what they don't seem to understand.

Eric: Whoever that chap was, the fact remains that I did what I did. And mother did what she did. And the rest of you did what you did to her. It's still the same rotten story whether it's been told to a police inspector or to somebody else. According to you, I ought to feel a lot better - (*To* Gerald.) I stole some money, Gerald, you might as well know - (*As* Birling *tries to interrupt.*) I don't care, let him know. The money's not the important thing. It's what happened to the girl and what we all did to her that matters. And I still feel the same about it, and that's why I don't feel like sitting down and having a nice cosy talk.

Sheila: And Eric's absolutely right. And it's the best thing any one of us has said tonight and it makes me feel a bit less ashamed of us. You're just beginning to pretend all over again.

Birling: Look – for God's sake!
Mrs Birling: (*protesting*) Arthur!
Birling: Well, my dear, they're so damned exasperating. They just won't try to understand our position or to see the difference between a lot of stuff like this coming out in a private and a downright public scandal.

Eric: (*shouting*) And I say the girl's dead and we all helped to kill her – and that's what matters -

Birling: (*also shouting, threatening* Eric) And I say – either stop shouting or get out.
(*Glaring at him but in quiet tone.*)
Some fathers I know would have kicked you out of the house anyhow by this time. So hold your tongue if you want to stay here.
Eric: (*quietly, bitterly*) I don't give a damn now whether I stay here or not.
Birling: You'll stay here long enough to give me an account of that money you stole – yes, and to pay it back too.
Sheila: But that won't bring Eva Smith back to life, will it?

Eric: And it doesn't alter the fact that we all helped to kill her.

His parent's coldness shocks him. Sheila agrees with him, and she is quite sympathetic when she says,

"That's just what I feel Eric. And it's what they don't seem to understand."

Eric emphatically points out that it's irrespective whether the Inspector was real or fake, but the fact remains that they all did do things that led to the girl's death. Sheila whole-heartedly agrees and tell Eric,

"And it's the best thing any one of us has said tonight."

And Sheila once more accuses her parents of pretending again,

"You're just beginning to pretend all over again."

Another argument ensues between Mr Birling and Eric. Mr Birling is worried about the 'public scandal' and Eric shouted,

"I say the girl's dead and we all helped to kill her."

Mr Birling shouts at Eric and he threatens him,

"Stop shouting or get out."

And he asks Eric to pay the money back. The situation has now become very tense.

Sheila defends Eric and tells her father that paying the money,

"won't bring Eva Smith back to life, will it?"

Eric is feeling remorse and guilt about Eva Smith's death and he insists that,

"It doesn't alter the fact that we all helped to kill her"

Gerald: But is it a fact?

Eric: Of course it is. You don't know the whole story yet.
Sheila: I suppose you're going to prove now you didn't spend last summer keeping this girl instead of seeing me eh?

Gerald: I did keep a girl last summer. I've admitted it. And I'm sorry, Sheila.

Sheila: Well, I must admit you came out of it better than the rest of us. The Inspector said that.

Birling: (*angrily*) He wasn't an Inspector.

Sheila: (*flaring up*) Well, he inspected us all right. And don't let's start dodging and pretending now. Between us we drove that girl to commit suicide.

Gerald: Did we? Who says so? Because I say – there's no more real evidence we did than there was that that chap was a police inspector.
Sheila: Of course there is.
Gerald: No, there isn't. Look at it. A and comes here pretending to be a police officer. It's a hoax of some kind. Now what does he do? Very artfully, working on bits of information he's picked up here and there, he bluffs us into confessing that we've all been mixed up in this girl's life in one way or another.
Eric: And so we have.
Gerald: But how do you know it's the same girl
Birling: (*eagerly*) Now wait a minute! Let's see how that would work. Now- (*hesitates*) no, it wouldn't.
Eric: We all admitted it.

END OF PART 13

Sheila seizes this opportunity to home in on Gerald's infidelity and she attacks him about his affair with Eva Smith. Gerald admits that he kept,

"a girl last summer"

and he apologises to Sheila.

Mr Birling angrily tells Sheila that,

"He wasn't an Inspector"

And Sheila flares up and tells her father off,

"Well, he inspected us all right. And don't let's start dodging and pretending now"

Sheila accuses her parents of pretending and denying the facts about Eva Smith's death.

START OF PART 14

Gerald: All right, you all admitted something to do with a girl. But how do you know it's the same girl?

// He looks round triumphantly at them. As they puzzle this out, he turns to Birling, *after pause. //*

Look here, Mr Birling. You sack a girl called Eva Smith. You've forgotten, but he shows you a photograph of her and then you remember. Right?

Birling: Yes, that part's straightforward enough. But what then?

Gerald: Well, then he happens to know that Sheila once had a girl sacked from Milward's shop. He tells us that it's this same Eva Smith. And he shows her a photograph that she recognizes.

Sheila: Yes. The same photograph.

Gerald: How do you know it's the same photograph? Did you see the one your father looked at?

Sheila: No, I didn't.

Gerald: And did you father see the one he showed you?

Sheila: No, he didn't. And I see what you mean now.

Gerald: We've no proof it was the same photograph and therefore no proof it was the same girl. Now take me. I never saw a photograph, remember. He caught me out by suddenly announcing that this girl changed her name to Daisy Renton, I gave myself away at once because I'd known a Daisy Renton.

Birling: (*eagerly*) And there wasn't the slightest proof that this Daisy Renton was really Eva Smith. We've only his word for it, and we'd his word for it that he was a police inspector, and we know now he was lying. So he could have been lying all the time.

Gerald: Of course, he could. Probably was. Now what happened after I left?

PHOTO of EVA SMITH and her DIARY

Gerald is trying to reason the Inspector's dealings; he was successful with convincing everyone except Eric. Gerald is doubting that it is the same girl that they were involved with.

Gerald queries the fact that none of them saw the photograph of Eva Smith together.

The Inspector ensured that each of them see the photograph individually. Gerald and Mr Birling concluded that the Inspector was lying.

ERIC

Mrs Birling: I was upset because Eric had left the house, and this man said that if Eric didn't come back, he'd have to go and find him. Well, that made me feel worse still. And his manner was so severe and he seemed so confident. Then quite suddenly he said I'd seen Eva Smith only two weeks ago.

Birling: Those were his exact words.
Mrs Birling: And like a fool I said Yes I had.
Birling: I don't see now why you did that. She didn't call herself Eva Smith when she came to see you at the committee, did she?

Mrs Birling: No, of course she didn't. But feeling so worried, when he suddenly turned on me with those questions, I answered more or less as he wanted me to answer.

Sheila: But, Mother, don't forget that he showed you a photograph of the girl before that, and you obviously recognized it.
Gerald: Did anybody else see it?
Mrs Birling: No, he showed it only to me.
Gerald: Then, don't you see, there's still no proof it was really the same girl. He might have showed you the photograph of any girl who applied to the committee. And how do we know she was really Eva Smith or Daisy Renton?
Birling: Gerald's dead right. He could have used a different photograph each time and we'd be none the wiser. We may all have been recognizing different girls.
Gerald: Exactly. Did he ask you to identify a photograph, Eric?
Eric: No. he didn't need a photograph by the time he'd got round to me. But obviously it must have been the girl I knew who went to see mother.
Gerald: Why must it?
Eric: She said she had to help because she wouldn't take any more stolen money. And the girl I knew had told me that already.

Gerald: Even then, that may have been all nonsense.

Mr and Mrs Birling gives Gerald a full explanation of the events that occurred when he was away. Mrs Birling complained about the Inspector's dominating personality which unnerved her.

"And his manner was so severe and he seemed so confident"

Mrs Birling admits that she was feeling so worried and that she,

"answered more or less as he wanted me to answer"

We can draw a contrast to her earlier entrance full of dismissiveness and confidence.

"Inspector I don't think we can help you"

Now she admits that the Inspector 'brought her to her knees' and she was compelled to do what he asked of her.

Gerald and Mr Birling joined forces and are laboriously trying to prove a point about it not being the same girl.

Actually, speaking their ridiculous point of argument has no relevance whatsoever because there was a girl who died and they have unwittingly contributed to her demise.

Gerald tries to get through to Eric and he asks him if he was asked to identify a photograph.

Eric is rather forthright and does not bow down to Gerald's pressure instead he stands up to him. Despite Eric telling him that all the facts relate to Eva Smith like the stolen money and that she went to see his mother, Gerald is still denying it.

"Even then, that may have been all nonsense"

It's obvious that Gerald is trying to act superior and knowledgeable, but Eric is not giving him the chance to do so.

TEXT	EXPLANATION
Eric: I don't see much nonsense about it when a girl goes and kills herself. You lot may be letting yourselves out nicely, but I can't. Nor can mother. We did her in all right.	He tells him very frankly that he does not see much nonsense about a girl committing suicide.
Birling: (*eagerly*) Wait a minute, wait a minute. Don't be in such a hurry to put yourself into court. That interview with your mother could have been just as much a put-up job, like all this police inspector business. The whole damned thing can have been a piece of bluff.	"You lot may be letting yourselves out nicely, but I can't" Mr Birling too is trying to deny the whole affair with the Inspector and insists that the interview with his wife was a bogus one.
Eric: (*angrily*) How can it? The girl's dead, isn't she? Gerald: What girl? There were probably four or five different girls.	"The whole damn thing can have been a piece of bluff" Eric is furious and he angrily questions his father, "How can it be? The girl's dead, isn't she? Gerald and Mr Birling is pursuing the fact that it could have been a different girl relentlessly, but Eric makes it clear,
Eric: That doesn't matter to me. The one I knew is dead.	"That doesn't matter to me. The one I knew is dead"
Birling: Is she? How do we know she is? Gerald: That's right. You've got it. How do we know any girl killed herself today? Birling: (*looking at them all, triumphantly*) Now answer that one. Let's look at it from this fellow's point of view. We're having a little celebration here and feeling rather pleased with ourselves. Now he has to work a trick on us. Well, the first thing he has to do is give us such a shock that after that he can bluff us all the time. So he starts right off. A girl has just died in the Infirmary. She drank some strong disinfectant. Died in agony-	Eric is clearly agitated and remorseful about Eva Smith's death. We can juxtapose his reaction to Gerald's and Mr Birling's selfish bigotry. Remember our hearts warmed towards Gerald because of his reaction to Eva Smith's death, despite him deserting her. He had so quickly forgot about the whole saga of Eva Smith's death and he is resuming his normal don't care attitude just like Mr and Mrs Birling.
Eric: All right, don't pile it on.	Mr Birling is very triumphant and he utters these words with not an ounce of regret or feeling in his theorizing of the events with the Inspector.
Birling: (*triumphantly*) There you are, you see. Just repeating it shakes you a bit. And that's what he had to do. Shake us at once – and then start questioning us – until we didn't know where we were. Oh – let's admit that. He had the laugh of us all right. Eric: He could laugh his head off – if I knew it really was all a hoax. Birling: I'm convinced it is. No police inquiry. No one girl that all this happened to. No scandal- Sheila: And no suicide? Gerald: (*decisively*) We can settle that at once.	"A girl has just died in the Infirmary. She drank some strong disinfectant. Died in agony-" Eric is very distraught and emotional, and he is angry with his father for displaying such ruthless behaviour in his unemotional description of Eva Smith. Eric says, "All right, don't pile it on"

Sheila: How?
Gerald: By ringing up the Infirmary. Either there's a dead girl there or there isn't.
Birling: (*uneasily*) It will look a bit queer, won't it – ringing up at this time of night-
Gerald: I don't mind doing it.
Mrs Birling: (*emphatically*) And if there isn't-

Gerald: Anyway we'll see. (*He goes to telephone and looks up number. The others watch tensely.*) Brumley eight nine eight six . . . Is that the Infirmary? This is Mr Gerald Croft – of Crofts Limited. . . . Yes. . . We're rather worried about one of our employees. Have you had a girl brought in this afternoon who committed suicide by drinking disinfectant – or any like suicide? Yes, I'll wait.

// *As he waits, the others show their nervous tension. Birling wipes his brow, Sheila shivers, Eric clasps and unclasps his hand, etc.*//

Yes? . . . You're certain of that. . . . I see. Well, thank you very much. . . Good night. (*He outs down telephone and looks at them.*) No girl has died in there today. Nobody's been brought in after drinking disinfectant. They haven't had a suicide for months.

Birling: (*triumphantly*) There you are! Proof positive. The whole story's just a lot of moonshine. Nothing but an elaborate sell! (*He produces a huge sigh of relief.*) Nobody likes to be sold as badly as that – but – for all that - (*he smiles at them all*) Gerald, have a drink.

Gerald: (*smiling*) Thanks, I think I could just do with one now.
Birling: (*going to sideboard*) So could I.

Mrs Birling: (*smiling*) And I must say, Gerald, you've argued this very cleverly, and I'm most grateful.

Gerald: (*going for his drink*) Well, you see, while I was out of the house I'd time to cool off and think things out a little.

Gerald decides to phone the infirmary to confirm whether there is a dead girl there or there isn't.

We are going to look at Gerald's unprofessional character throughout the play. Priestley is pointing out to us that Mrs Birling wrongfully attributed lying to the lower social classes like Eva Smith but the hypocrisy here is that both Mr Birling and Gerald, both from the rich capitalist class are lying through their teeth as though it is normal, acceptable behaviour. When Gerald phones the infirmary, to enquire if any girl who committed suicide was brought in, he lies again,

"We are rather worried about one of our employees"

The Birling's are very nervous whilst waiting in anticipation for the news. 'Birling wipes his brow; Sheila shivers and Eric clasps and unclasps his hands'.

Mr Birling is triumphant when Gerald confirms that,

"No girl has died in there today"

Mr Birling dismisses the whole saga about Eva Smith and the Inspector as a lot of nonsense,

"The whole story's just a lot of moonshine"

It's rather surprising that Mr and Mrs Birling came to know about Gerald's infidelity with Eva Smith. This is obviously a dent to Sheila's confidence and has caused her pain, yet Mr and Mrs Birling are so quick to embrace Gerald. One can argue that the relationship between Gerald and Sheila is more like a business merger that a love relationship.

Mr and Mrs Birling seem to be enamoured by Gerald, Mrs Birling says,

"And I must say Gerald, you've argued this very cleverly, and I am most grateful"

In contrast, Eric has accepted responsibility for his actions and have gained the respect and the admiration of the audience.

Birling: *(giving him a drink)* Yes, he didn't keep you on the run as he did the rest of us. I'll admit now he gave me a bit of a scare at the time. But I'd a special reason for not wanting any public scandal just now. *(Has his drink now, and raises his glass.)* Well, here's to us. Come on, Sheila, don't look like that. All over now.

Sheila: The worst part is. But you're forgetting one thing I still can't forget. Everything we said had happened really had happened. If it didn't end tragically, then that's lucky for us. But it might have done.

Birling: *(jovially)* But the whole thing's different now. Come, come, you can see that, can't you? *(Imitating Inspector in his final speech.)* You all helped to kill her. *(pointing at Sheila and Eric, and laughing.)* and I wish you could have seen the look on your faces when he said that.

// Sheila moves towards door. //

Going to bed, young woman?

Sheila: *(tensely)* I want to get out of this. It frightens me the way you talk.

Birling: *(heartily)* Nonsense! You'll have a good laugh over it yet. Look, you'd better ask Gerald for that ring you gave back to him, hadn't you? Then you'll feel better.

Sheila: *(passionately)* You're pretending everything's just as it was before.

Eric: I'm not!
Sheila: No, but these others are.
Birling: Well, isn't it? We've been had, that's all.
Sheila: So nothing really happened. So there's nothing to be sorry for, nothing to learn.
We can all go on behaving just as we did.
Mrs Birling: Well, why shouldn't we?
Sheila: I tell you – whoever that Inspector was, it was anything but a joke. You knew it then. You began to learn something. And now you've stopped. You're ready to go on in the same old way.

Gerald is all pompous and is taking the lead in solving the case but earlier he wanted to do a runner to avoid the Inspector's questioning. He phones the infirmary and enquires whether a girl was brought in who committed suicide by drinking disinfectant. Priestley creates a lot of tension and suspense here. Not only are the audience dying of suspense but the characters themselves are tense and curious as shown by their body language. Anyway, the infirmary confirms that there wasn't any girl who died of a suicide in the infirmary. Now they are all celebrating this news with a drink. But Sheila doesn't share in their excitement. She still insists that everything they said had happened.

MR ARTHUR BIRLING triumphant after calling the infirmary.

Sheila gets up to go and says,

"It frightens me the way you talk?"

Mr Birling is jovial and hearty,

"You'll have a good laugh over it."

He tells Sheila to take the ring back from Gerald. Once again, Sheila says,
"You're pretending everything's just as it was before."

She is so angry that her parents are carrying on as normal, as though nothing has happened clearly portraying the characteristics of the Capitalist class,
"You're ready to go on in the same old way.

Birling: *(amused)* And you're not, eh?

Sheila: No, because I remember what he said, how he looked, and what he made me feel. Fire and blood and anguish. And it frightens me the way you talk, and I can't listen to any more of it.

Eric: And I agree with Sheila. It frightens me too.
Birling: Well, go to bed then, and don't stand there being hysterical.

Mrs Birling: They're over-tired. In the morning they'll be as amused as we are.

Gerald: Everything's all right now, Sheila. *(Holds up the ring.)* What about this ring?
Sheila: No, not yet. It's too soon. I must think.

Birling: *(pointing to Eric and Sheila)* Now look at the pair of them – the famous younger generation who know it all. And they can't even take a joke-

// The telephone rings sharply. There is a moment's complete silence. Birling goes to answer it. //

Yes?. . . Mr Birling speaking. . . .What? - here-

//But obviously the other person has rung off. He puts the telephone down slowly and looks in a panic-stricken fashion at the others. //

Birling: That was the police. A girl has just died – on her way to the Infirmary – after swallowing some disinfectant. And a police inspector is on his way here – to ask some – questions -----

// As they stare guiltily and dumbfounded, the curtain falls. //

END OF PART 14

END OF ACT THREE

END OF PLAY

She repeats the Inspector's words,

"Fire and blood and anguish"

And surely, she has learnt something from this powerful speech about redemption and remorse. Mrs Birling is very composed when she says,

"They are over-tired. In the morning they'll be as amused as we are."
Mr Birling refers to Eric and Sheila as,

"the famous younger generation who know it all"

Sheila and Eric behaved exactly how Priestley wanted them to behave and be a stepping stone for future social mobility.

In conclusion the symbol of ringing surfaces again. Now it's the telephone that rings sharply. Once again, Priestley creates suspense because there is a moment of complete silence and Mr birling is once more panic-stricken after he puts the phone down. He tells everyone that the police had called, and a girl had died after drinking some disinfectant and a police inspector is on his way here to ask some questions. As they all stare guiltily and dumbfounded, the curtain falls.

| GERALD | ERIC | SYBIL | GOOLE | ARTHUR | SHEILA |

GOOLE	ACT 1	ARTHUR	SYBIL	ACT 1	SHEILA	GERALD	ERIC
	Part 1			Part 1			
	Part 2			Part 2			
	Part 3			Part 3			
	Part 4			Part 4			
	Part 5			Part 5			

GOOLE	ACT 2	ARTHUR	SYBIL	ACT 2	SHEILA	GERALD	ERIC
	Part 6			Part 6			
	Part 7			Part 7			
	Part 8			Part 8			
	Part 9			Part 9			

GOOLE	ACT 3	ARTHUR	SYBIL	ACT 3	SHEILA	GERALD	ERIC
	Part 10			Part 10			
	Part 11			Part 11			
	Part 12			Part 12			
	Part 13			Part 13			
	Part 14			Part 14			

INSPECTOR GOOLE

Inspector Goole is an omniscient, mysterious, supernatural character. He is a thought-provoking character who is Priestley's mouthpiece and the Inspector echoes Priestley's socialist views of moral obligation, social responsibility, and social justice. The main theme of responsibility is epitomised by the Inspector's use of biblical imagery in his final speech,

"We don't live alone. We are members of one body."

meaning that like Christ who died for the World, we should help the less fortunate, like Eva Smith in Society. Priestley harboured an innate empathy for the poorer socialist class and the social inequality in Britain during the Edwardian era which weighed heavily on his mind hence he used the Inspector to convey his message.

The Inspector's arrival signals a very important twist to the play. The soft, pink, and intimate lighting changes to be brighter and harder evoking a tone change and signalling the terrible news he brings and foreshadows the conflict to follow within the Birling family. The change also denotes the power and importance of the Inspector in initiating this conflict and steering it towards justice for Eva Smith.

He also enters at the opportune moment, with the sharp ring of the doorbell when Mr Birling was giving Eric and Gerald a very selfish message,

"A man has to mind his own business and look after himself, - Their family because the way some of these cranks talk, - As if we were all mixed up together like bees in a hive."

He also comes dressed in a plain, darkish suit bringing dark news. He is also described as a very dominating, charismatic person who creates an impression of 'massiveness, solidity and purposefulness,' speaking carefully and weightily. He remains solid and sturdy although he was intimidated by Mr and Mrs Birling. This charismatic character helps to move the plot along and with his,

"One person and one line of enquiry at a time"

He manages to control the development of events and with his commanding attitude was able to virtually bring the Birlings' to their knees. He had the biggest impact on Sheila who was mesmerised with the Inspector, and she seemed to have switched sides hence helping the Inspector with his investigation, urging the other family members to listen to him and says,

"Don't build walls between us and the Inspector, otherwise he will only break you down"

She reacted very passionately and with remorse when the Inspector revealed her role in Eva Smith's death. She gives a half-stifled sob and then runs out. Even Eric is impressed with the Inspector, and he acknowledges responsibly for his actions. Priestley intended for the younger generation to be his vision for the future. Unlike the older generation who refused to accept their responsibility and try to defend their actions. Mrs Birling said,

"But I accept no blame for it at all."

The Inspector was very firm in his dealings with the Birlings. He targeted their conscience and set the cat among the pigeons because they started to fight among themselves,

"Don't stammer and yammer at me again man. I am losing all patience with you people."

From that bold, arrogant first entrance, we now see a very humiliated, 'rather cowed' Mrs Birling during her questioning by the Inspector. He also attacks their guilty conscience by presenting them timeously with a vivid, graphic image of Eva Smith's death.

"She lies with a burnt-out inside on a slab."

He deliberately depicts this scene so that the Birlings can actually visualise the scene and acknowledge the error of their ways and act more socially responsible in future. Priestley uses him as a catalyst to deliver his message of social responsibility and moral ethnics. Priestley presents the Inspector as one who is overpowering and enigmatic. During his interrogations of the characters, he is blunt and exerts his authority when there is dissention between the members of the family. He also employs unique methods of questioning and interrogation. For example, he shows the photographs to one person at a time, hence creating a lot of suspense and tension, arousing the curiosity of the audience. Priestley presents the Inspector as very gallant and confident character who is not intimidated by social status. Mrs Birling accuses him of conducting his enquiry in,

"a rather peculiar and offensive manner"

She also threatens him with her status in society,

"You know my husband was Lord mayor only two years ago and that he's still magistrate."

This of course didn't deter the Inspector one bit. Priestley describes the Inspector as 'Purposefulness', suggesting that he is there to effectively and explicitly 'do his duty' of educating the Birlings from the Capitalist class to become more aware of the consequences of their actions and develop a sense of responsibility towards the socialist class. Even Mr Birling gives into the Inspector's suggestion about giving Eric a drink after he refused him one. The Inspector connects with each person, psychologically pressuring them to open up and take responsibility.

Towards the end this all-imposing Inspector takes charge masterfully when he yells 'STOP!', to quell the Birling squabble. The exclamation mark suggesting his authority. They all became quiet, staring at him. His power in controlling the Birlings is evident here. He goes on to once again, target their conscience when he declares,

"But each of you helped to kill her"

He then singles out each one and reminds them of their role in Eva Smith's death. Even Mr Birling felt horrible and offered money.

"Look Inspector – I'd give thousands – yes, thousands"

To which the Inspector replies that it is too late now. His parting speech is very poignant and powerful when he says that,

"One Eva Smith has gone – but there are millions and millions of Eva Smiths left with us"

He is talking about the millions of underprivileged, poor socialist class proletariats who are trampled on by the rich capitalist class. He further emphasis that,

"We are responsible for each other"

The Inspector ends his visit with a very threatening message intended to jolt the Birlings into acting socially responsible. If they don't do this, he warns them,

"they will be taught it in fire and blood and anguish"

He uses biblical imagery reminding them of God's wrath and their punishment of fire and brimstone at the end of their lives.

MR ARTHUR BIRLING

Priestley very carefully crafted Mr Birling who is depicted as an obnoxious, egotistical and brazen character, a privileged product of the aristocratic class values. Mr Birling represented the rich, capitalist class of the Edwardian era who profited from the poor socialist class like Eva Smith, vying for

"lower costs and higher prices"

Priestley's distaste of the capitalist class is enhanced by his use of the bitter tone when describing Mr Birling.

He describes him as a prosperous businessman who is very pompous about being Lord Mayor and he boasts about his impending knighthood which will ensure his climb up the social ladder.

Mr Birling is also described as a 'heavy - looking, portentous man in his middle fifties with fairly easy manners'. By his constant reference to status,

"hard-headed businessman"

we can gage that he is a man obsessed with power and social status.

He is beaming with pride that Sheila is marrying into a rich, aristocratic family like the Crofts who are socially superior to the Birlings. He desires to be on par with the Crofts and this is evident when he mentions to Gerald that he purchased the same wine like his father did, implying that he is somewhat reaching Mr Croft's status. The stage directions describe his speech as rather provincial suggesting that he is not so esteemed or socially connected as the Crofts who see him as socially inferior because he wasn't born rich but acquired his money through hard work. He can be referred to as "new money," which does not entitle him to fit into the aristocracy.

Mr Birling puffs up with pride when he tells Gerald that his engagement to Sheila means a "tremendous lot" to him.

"You're just the kind of son-in-law I always want"

A merger with the Crofts and the Birlings would be ideal to help Mr Birling to climb the social ladder. He is thrilled that he will no longer be competing but are now business partners working together. Once again, his avaricious nature is highlighted because it's evident that he wants to make money at the expense of the poor socialist class like Eve Smith. He regrets that the Crofts are absent from the engagement.

"It's a pity Sir George and - we - Lady Croft can't be with us"

One can assume that they were deliberately absent because the Birlings are socially inferior to them, and they want to show their discontent about this union between Sheila and Gerald. Mr Birling also tells Gerald that he knows that his parents think that he is engaged to a girl, who is 'not good enough'. Mr Birling's house is described as 'heavily comfortable but not cosy and homelike' and Mr Birling is described as 'heavy looking'. This description of inanimate objects can be associated with Mr Birling's cold, unfeeling nature. He is also seen as very unfriendly and unapproachable as Eric confirms,

"You are not the kind of father a chap can go to when he's in trouble"

Priestly suggests that Mr Birling is also very threatening and imposing in his behaviour during his liaison with the inspector. During his speeches with the boys, the repeated use of the alliteration 'hard-headed businessman', repeatedly suggesting his desperate rise on the social ladder.

When he meets the Inspector, he assumes a position of importance and flaunts his social status,

"I was Lord Mayor"

clearly intended to threaten and intimidate the inspector. His initial speech to Eric and Gerald,

"A man has to mind his own business and look after his own"

reeks of selfishness which Eric points out to him later in the play, implying that his father taught him to be selfish,

"I didn't notice that you told him that it's every man for himself"

He also clearly displays a sense of racial prejudices as seen in his cruel attack on the people from the East,

"half civilized folks in the Balkans"
And
"Russia which will always be behindhand naturally"

His glaring selfishness and lack of social mobility is quite evident when he says we should not be,

"mixed up together like bees in a hive"

Priestley's use of this animal imagery clearly depicts Mr Birling's contempt of Socialism adopted by the privileged capitalist class. He also shows no empathy for the poor socialist class because he didn't even acknowledge his employees and Eva Smith's photograph was unrecognisable to him at first. We are made aware of his individualistic and capitalist views when he lays out the details for his reasons for firing her for

"lower costs and higher profits"

He looked down upon the poorer social class whom he deemed as morally and socially inferior and saw them as cheap labour.

When Eric rebukes him for firing Eva Smith, he attacks Eric's public school and varsity life. Eric is portrayed by Priestley as an amiable character here who is in direct contrast to his father who, recons that this whole business with Eva Smith is,

"rather awkward"

Hence, we can safely say that Eric was Priestley's vision for the future because he displays a certain empathy and social responsibility towards the proletariats. Even Sheila questions and condemns her father's behaviour and displays a consciousness of social responsibility

"But those girls aren't cheap labour – they're people"

Sheila's impassioned plea also suggest that she too was Priestley's vision for the future to change Edwardian Britain's aristocratic, individualistic, and acquisitive nature.

Mr Birling's self-inflated and pompous attitude creates a conflict between the inspector's calm yet powerful presence. He fiercely protects his family's well-being which is evident during his furious outburst with the Inspector,

"I protest against the way in which my daughter, a young unmarried girl, is being dragged into this"

The use of the pronoun 'my' suggesting his selfishness which can mirror his,

"A man has to look after himself and his family"

Priestley once again maps out for the audience and society of the 1946 Edwardian era that these types of selfish prejudices and lack of social mobility cannot be tolerated, and that a fair and drastic social change is needed. His intervention is also poignant when the inspector questions Mrs Birling,

"Is there any reason why my wife should answer questions?"

Once again, we see his overwhelming protectiveness of his family, yet he displayed a total disrespect and lack of responsibility for Eva Smith's pathetic situation.

His dramatic response when he heard that Eva Smith called herself,

"Mrs Birling"

was an angry retort with a shocked exclamation,

"Damned impudence!"

His furious outburst when he hears about Eric's affair,

"I don't want any talk from you"

and he was livid when he heard that Eric had the audacity to steal money from the company. Tensions rise dramatically when Eric verbally attacks his mother and Mr Birling almost gets physical with Eric and angrily intervenes,

"Why you, hysterical young fool-get back-or I'll"

Typical of his capitalistic views and his desire to maintain his social status Mr Birling focuses wholly on avoiding a scandal.

In a dramatic final twist, the Inspector warns him that people will pay in

"fire and blood and anguish"

if they blindly and arrogantly ignore their social responsibility. At the end we see that Mr Birling has made no significant change and totally ignored the Inspector's poignant warning message. He very arrogantly states,

"it's all over now"
And
"You will have a good laugh over it"

Obviously, Mr Birling has shown no remorse for his actions and has learnt nothing from this experience. He resumed his normal selfish capitalist lifestyle and pretended that nothing had happened.

MRS SYBIL BIRLING

Mrs Birling is portrayed by Priestley as the typical aristocratic Capitalist class woman who is the embodiment of social class and snobbery. Priestley's description of her hints at his anger towards the avariciousness of the Capitalist class during the Edwardian Era,

> "A rather cold woman who was her husband's social superior"

Priestley writes with a bitter tone whilst portraying Mrs Birling in a negative light thus ensuring that the audience sees through her hypocrisy and her superficiality and see her downfall as a triumph.

Her home was described as, 'not cosy and homelike', suggesting that she was cold and unfriendly like her home because of her staunch capitalist beliefs. Priestley associates her ostentatious, character to that of her house which is an inanimate object - cold and lifeless. She was unsympathetic and out of touch with the sufferings of the poor working classes like Eva Smith and her shocking prejudices against her when she was desperate for her help astounds the audience.

She used her position of superiority and authority to turn down her plea for help simply because she used the title, 'Mrs Birling', calling it,

> "impertinence"

Mrs Birling is more concerned about her social status and show a complete lack of social responsibility towards Eva Smith's situation. She is ruthless when she says,

"I accept no blame for it all"

She is so egocentric that she doesn't accept any blame and she very indignantly use several euphemisms, indicating that Eva Smith is morally inferior to her,

"girl of that sort"

Her sense of hypocrisy is quite evident here when she claims,

"We help deserving cases"

Ironically Eva Smith was a very deserving case indeed but was not given any help. Mrs Birling's snobbery is also evident at the beginning of the play, when she reprimands Mr Birling for congratulating the cook,

"Arthur you are not supposed to say such things"

When she confronts the Inspector, she slips into the room in a very easy, confident manner displaying her very privileged position. We see a lack of perception when she foolishly tells the Inspector,

"I don't think we can help you very much"

When the Inspector revealed the purpose of his visit about Eva Smith's death, she refers to it as "absurd business"

Here Priestley is highlighting the selfish attitude of the Edwardian ruling class.

Priestley builds dramatic tension when Mrs Birling says that the father should be held responsible and that he should confess in public, and her lack of perception makes her squirm when she learns that Eric is the father. She thought that she was indestructible because of her superior status and wealth. Her short-sightedness didn't allow her to see beyond the confines of her drawing room and her social position.

She was unable to detect that her son was an alcoholic and that he was responsible for fathering Eva Smith's child and insists that he,

"ought to be dealt with severely"

Despite Sheila's urgent pleas for her mother to stop,

> "No mother please!"

she simply ignores Sheila and continues her tirade of threatening the Inspector. When the Inspector accuses her of showing no compassion to Eva Smith,

> "you slammed the door in her face"

she maintains her composure and speaks in a rather dramatic fashion insisting that it was the girl's fault. Her lack of social mobility and her arrogant capitalist views forces her to deny any responsibility. Priestley creates suspense and tension, and the audience is curious to see Mrs Birling's reaction when the truth about Eric being the father is unravelled. Of course, she is in denial once again,

> "I don't believe it. I won't believe it"

Eric became furious with his mother for her prejudiced and horrible treatment of Eva Smith. He accuses her of killing her own grandchild,

> "You killed them both"

She is practically on her fours begging Eric for forgiveness insisting that she didn't know it was him. Sadly though, in the end she is unrepentant, and she resumes her life as normal and is happy to resume her capitalistic beliefs. Priestley shows his deep concern for this shallow Edwardian ruling class behaviour, and his hope for a more equal society where socialist values are embraced, are fast diminishing.

Sheila shows her disgust for her mother's behaviour,

> "you are ready to go on in the same old way"

Mrs Birling's lack of empathy and conscience disgusts the audience,

> "In the morning they will be as amused as we are"

She obviously learnt nothing and the Inspector's message,

> "In fire, blood and anguish"

did not deter her one bit.

SHEILA BIRLING

Sheila's significance and the transformation in her character in the play, portrays Priestley's hope that a better socially responsible society can emerge in Post War Britain. Sheila is the only character carefully crafted by Priestley to be used as the voice of the people's conscience. As the play progresses there is a gradual, steady development in her character. She is Priestley's vision for the future and a vehicle for Priestley's strong, socialist views.   Sheila is presented as an amiable and considerate character.

"Sheila is a pretty girl in her early twenties, very pleased with life and rather excited"

Ironically, if we trace Priestley's stage directions, we see her excitement change to distress as the events about Eva Smith's death unfold. Initially, Priestley presents her as a typically spoilt, privileged daughter of the Capitalist Aristocratic class.

At the beginning of the play, she is depicted as being immature and carefree, very child-like,

> "I am listening, daddy"

She's also enamoured with superficial things like clothes and the ring. Sheila abused her status and her wealth to get Eva Smith fired, because she was overwrought with jealously. Priestley is trying to emphasise how the rich, capitalist class was out of touch with the sufferings of the poor socialist class. Sheila was oblivious of the impact her wrath will have because her action of getting Eva Smith fired unleashed a chain of events which ultimately led to her death.

The irony of the situation is that her boyfriend Gerald had to remedy her mess by providing Eva Smith with love and protection when she was homeless and hungry. The Inspector's arrival has drastically changed Sheila from an energetic young girl who uses slang expressions like,

"squiffy"

to a strong mature lady whose reactions to Eva Smith's death is a far cry to that of the older generation. She is deeply saddened to learn of her role in Eva Smith's death and she assumes full responsibility for her actions,

"I know I am to blame"

The acknowledgement of her action can be juxtaposed to that of Mrs Birling

"I don't think we can help you much"

and Mr Birling's,

"If you don't come down sharply on some of these people, they'd soon be asking for the earth"

Sheila is also totally disturbed at her mother's behaviour towards the Inspector, and she urges her mother to stop,

"It's crazy, stop it Mother"

She is clearly disturbed and show genuine remorse and she wants her mother to listen to the inspector. Her display of deep sympathy for Eva Smith's situation startles the audience to see such a significant change in Sheila and she gradually wins the audience's admiration and respect.

The Inspector has had a huge influence on her and she seems to be slowly creeping towards the Inspector's ways of thinking and morals. Hence, trying desperately to educate her parents to see the error of their ways. She even helps the inspector to point out her parent's failings leaving her mother horrified. She also warns Gerald,

"I hate to think how much he knows that we don't know yet"

Her fascination and awe about the Inspector, highlights her sense of perception because later on in the play she was the only one who questions who he was.

When Gerald asked her to leave, she was adamant and refused to go, Sheila's strength is gaining momentum. Since the play is a morality play, Sheila is taking stock of her morals because she is very impressed with Gerald's honesty despite what he had done. Her sense of maturity is evident here because she urges everybody to be honest and accept responsibility. Breaking off her engagement with Gerald was a rather bold move knowing full well that her parents would not welcome the idea, after all we can assume this union was more like a business deal.

Sheila's strength, maturity and sincerity in her development is making her more like the inspector who she views as a very superior being. At the beginning of the play, she jokes with Gerald but the stage directions say that she is,

"half-serious, half-playful"

We can gage that beneath that childishness, she harboured 'serious' concerns about her relationship with Gerald. These concerns proved to materialise later in the play when she discovered Gerald's affair. Priestley gives Sheila lots of witty and sometimes funny lines,

"Well we didn't think you meant Buckingham Palace"

making her appear sharp and alert. Her wit simply undermined the authority of the others because she started asking questions just like the Inspector. Unlike the others Sheila acknowledges that she used her power to get Eva Smith fired and she is willing to atone for her behaviour and learn from the consequences. She contradicts and undermines her parent's behaviour just the way the inspector does.

When she gives the ring back to Gerald, she boldly tells her father,

"Don't interfere"

Sheila see that the inspector attacks the others confidence by bombarding them with a series of questions. He does this to break down the 'wall' which they have built between themselves and Eva Smith. Sheila wants to do the same. Her bold stance shocks the audience especially when she tells Eric that their mother refused to help Eva Smith. Sheila wants everyone's bad deeds to be exposed and hopefully have them redeem themselves, unfortunately they did not. She is horrified that Gerald and her parents had resumed their normal lives as before, at the end of the play. She wanted them to stop their,

"silly pretences"

She passionately reprimands her parents,

> "You're are pretending everything's just as it was before"

When Gerald asks her to take the ring back, Sheila, we see is no more the naïve, young girl anymore but tells Gerald,

> "No, not yet. It's too soon. I must think."

Priestley uses Sheila as a moral judge at the end of the play. She says,

> "probably between us we killed her"

yet the others don't get as far as admitting that.

The portrayal of Sheila's character in the play is exactly what Priestley envisioned for the rigid, selfish Edwardian society of 1912. He wanted the younger generation to pioneer his new morality in politics and assume social responsibility for the poorer social class and to be a vehicle to herald a new dawn in capitalist Edwardian Britain.

ERIC BIRLING

Priestley's depiction of Eric's character is juxtaposed to that of Gerald's. They seem to be conflicting characters although from the same Capitalist playground. Both play a very different role in upholding Priestley's passionate message of social responsibility.
Eric is described as being in his,

"early twenties not quite at ease, half shy, half-assertive."

Eric belongs to the younger generation, and he is Priestley's vision for the future to encourage social mobility among the Capitalist Class of the Edwardian Era. Although he is portrayed as a classic example of how the spoilt, privileged young men of the capitalist class, who exploit and manipulate girls from the underprivileged social class, Eric did show many redeeming qualities.

Priestley's description of Eric is quite apt because he is portrayed as being insecure and not too confident. One can attribute this to the fact that he and his father shared a very detached and distant relationship. It's obvious that Gerald occupies a more affectionate and acceptable place in Mr Birling's heart than Eric does. When Mr Birling asked him why he didn't come to him for help, Eric's sad response was that he was,

"not the kind of father a chap can go to when he is in trouble."

In a drunken stupor Eric got Eva Smith pregnant and tried to make amends by stealing his father's money to support her, thereby accepting responsibility for his actions. Just like all the privileged Capitalist class children, Eric had the superior public school and varsity education. When Mr Birling was irate with Eric when he stood up to him and defended Eva Smith,

"Why shouldn't they try for higher wages?"

Mr Birling accuses Eric of not learning anything from varsity which,

"doesn't seem to teach you"

The poignancy in which Eric enters and exits is a deliberate ploy by Priestley to create suspense. Eric enters at a strategic point in the play, after everyone had learnt that he is the father of Eva Smith's child. The tension is so palpable and even the audience becomes tense because they want to see his parent's reaction. He feels guilty and empathetic for Eva Smith's death. His reaction is rather emotive,

"We all helped to kill her"

The use of the collective noun shows that they were all equally to blame for the horrible death of Eva Smith; it was not only Eric's action which culminated in her death. Sheila tells him that his mother has been blaming everything on the young man who got this girl into trouble. Eric becomes furious with his mother and tells her,

"You haven't made it any easier for me, have you, Mother?"

He also accuses her of misunderstanding him and he threatened her, verbally attacking her, to the horror of Mr Birling,

"You killed them both"

We witness Eric's pain and suffering when he dramatically utters,

"Oh – my – God! How stupid it all is!"

This fragmented sentence with dashes and the repeated exclamation marks show how very distressed and remorseful he was for his actions. It detects his loss of control because his words didn't have the normal, regimented flow. His reaction bodes well for Priestley's hope and dreams for the younger generation to take social responsibility. His genuine concern can be juxtaposed to that of his parents cold, arrogant response to Eva Smith's death. Both Eric and Sheila acknowledge that despite the inspector being a 'hoaxer,' they are still guilty of Eva Smith's death because they have acted exactly as the Inspector had accused them of, which led to Eva Smith's death.

Although one can argue that Eric exploited Eva Smith, the audience tend to empathise and forgive his indiscretions. The fact that his mother didn't know about his drinking habits is testimony enough to show how detached she was from her son. At times he expressed frustration and desperation and he also did something immoral by stealing money to give to Eva Smith. Despite that, the audience has a certain respect for his actions because he attempted to take responsibility for his actions and just didn't desert her. Mr Birling tells him that he has to repay the money that he had stolen. We also tend to admire Eric's boldness because he tells his parents that he is ashamed of them. We see a rapid development in his strength of character. At the end of the play, we see a dramatic change in Eric and we can juxtapose it to Gerald's arrogant attitude about responsibility. He began to change his ideas and values and have become more aware of his faults, and he is prepared to make amends and take responsibility for his actions. When Sheila accuses him of
"pretending everything's just as it was before"

he denies it and agrees with Sheila about his parent's pretences and concludes by saying,
"I agree with Sheila. It frightens me too."

GERALD CROFT

Priestley describes Gerald Croft as,

"very much the well-bred, man about town"

Priestley's vision for the younger generation to be symbols of hope and assume social responsibility was expected of Gerald because he belonged to the highest hierarchy on the social ladder. Because of his social and economic status, it was very easy for him to bring about social mobility in Post war Britain, yet he chose to shun his social responsibility. Gerald represented the son of a typical aristocratic class in Edwardian Society.

Very often Gerald agrees with Mr Birling's capitalistic views. Priestley uses vivid adjectives, 'attractive' and 'well bred' to emphasise his life of privilege and power. He is of high social standing and being a man 'about town', embarked on his sordid affair with Eva Smith. He upholds his belief in capitalism and although he is young, he aligns himself with the beliefs of the older generation and he refuses to accept responsibility for his actions. He wanted to sneak away when he realised that the Inspector was going to target him about his affair with Eva Smith.

He is the direct opposite of Eric and seem to be seen as being more favourable to Mr Birling than Eric was. When Mr Birling gives his capitalistic talk about protecting,

"the interests of capital"

Gerald readily agrees,

"I believe you're right sir"

Mr Birling develops a cordial relationship with Gerald because his family is more socially superior to the Birling's, and he sees social status and his business contacts as advantageous. Mr Birling is excited that there will be a merger between the Birlings and the Crofts businesses. Being contemporaries Gerald ought to have befriended Eric but he chose to make fun of Eric with Mr Birling,

"Unless Eric's been up to something"

Ironically Eric is rather annoyed at Gerald's statement, but Mr Birling gets angry with Eric for telling Gerald off.

Hence, we see a distance in the relationship between Eric and his father. Mr Birling tells Gerald of his impending knighthood in secret and Gerald congratulates him on his success. He also justifies Mr Birling's sacking of Eva Smith,

"You couldn't have done anything else"

It's clear that his capitalist upbringing enables him to reject the socialist views of Social responsibility, just like Mr Birling. He too achieved his wealth and success by exploiting the poor Socialist class like Eva Smith. Priestley's description of Gerald's attitude is a direct attack on the avaricious nature of capitalism.

When the Inspector reveals Gerald's role in Eva Smith's death, Gerald didn't want Sheila to witness details of his affair with Eva Smith,

"It's bound to be unpleasant and disturbing"

He didn't want this affair to jeopardise his relationship with Sheila. Once again protecting his self-interest. Since Gerald showed some responsibility towards Eva Smith to an extent, he said that he,

"was sorry for her because she was desperately hard up

He seemed to have won the affections of the Inspector and Sheila's admiration of him for his honesty. He was also genuinely distressed and emotional when he realised that she is dead and he says that he is,

"more - upset - by this business than I probably appear to be"

The use of the hyphens tells us that Gerald is over emotional, and this fragmented statement show that his speech is not flowing, and he is perhaps suppressing his emotions. He then goes for a walk to try to calm down.

Gerald boldly tells Mrs Birling that his affair with Eva Smith was not 'disgusting.' He speaks affectionately of her and says that she was 'gallant' when their relationship ended. The audience feels a sense of sympathy for Gerald because he demonstrates a deep and genuine remorse for his actions, and he also said that he

"Made her happy for a time"

Of course, Gerald's affair with Eva Smith has both pros and cons because it can be argued that although he helped her and has shown genuine remorse, he also cheated on Sheila and had an illegitimate affair with Eva Smith knowing full well that he was not going to marry her.

Sheila took a bold stance when she broke off her engagement with Gerald and she signalled Priestley's vision for the future. Coming from a patriarchal society and knowing full well how her father cherished this union – to him it was more of a business contract, yet she rejects it because of Gerald's lack of social responsibility and moral judgements. She is a symbol of hope and Priestley wants the next generation to become socially responsible and build a better society for the proletariats. Priestley hopes that the Capitalists ideals and their avaricious nature should be quelled. In the end Gerald shows insight, to the admiration of Mrs Birling when he 'very cleverly' discovers that the inspector's claims were fabricated, and he phones the infirmary to confirm Eva Smith's suicide.

However, in the end Gerald proves to be just like the Birling's because he is content that life has resumed to normal. He still followed his Capitalist ideals and learnt nothing from the experience. He holds up the ring and says,

"Everything is all right now Sheila"

EVA SMITH alias Daisy Renton
(later as) alias Mrs Birling

Because Eva Smith was a woman in Edwardian Britain where women were not yet awarded the right to vote – she was in an even worse position than a lower-class man. Even upper-class women had few choices because they had no real status. They had to impress a rich man and marry well like Sheila Birling.

Eva Smith alias Daisy Renton (and later as) alias Mrs Birling never appears on stage, yet she plays a pivotal role in moving the plot along. Priestley very carefully constructed this sympathetic character whose pathetic situation tugs at the heartstrings of the audience. She represents the working class – proletariat who were exploited by the Capitalist class during the Edwardian Era. Sadly, much to Priestley's chagrin there are,

> "Millions and millions and millions of Eva Smith's"

Priestley portrays the Birling's and Gerald Croft as vile, opportunistic, and self-indulgent individuals who bear no social responsibility because of their privileged status. He hits out at the Birling's and Gerald by writing with a bitter tone about Eva Smith's suffering.

The Inspector, very sympathetically describes her in a very positive light as,

> "very pretty with a promising life"

The fact that all the other characters discuss her life and fate without her being present gives us an indication of how the poor Socialist Class, during the Edwardian Era had no voice and could not challenge the Capitalist Class.

Eva Smith couldn't challenge Mrs Birling who accused her of being,

> "impertinent"

and

> "the girl who had been causing trouble in the works"

was Mr Birling's accusation. Mrs Birling's constant use of euphemisms,

> "girl of that sort"

to describe Eva Smith highlighting Mrs Birling's superior moral stance because she certainly looked down upon Eva Smith as being morally and socially inferior to her.

Mrs Birling's arrogance is clearly evident because she refused Eva Smith's plea for help over something so trivial like using the Birling's name. Her shallowness and lack of empathy for the sufferings of the poor socialist class portray her as a typical cold, aristocratic, capitalist female who totally lacks social responsibility. Her hypocrisy and selfishness are further enhanced when she says that,

> "We help deserving cases."

knowing full well that Eva Smith was poor and vulnerable.

Mrs Birling also couldn't believe that Eva Smith refused to take money from Eric because it was stolen and

> "a girl of that sort"

according to Mrs Birling's prejudiced view would never refuse money because Eva Smith belonged to the social class who would do anything to acquire money.

Eva Smith portrayed a dignity that Mrs Birling's clouded perception of her couldn't comprehend. Gerald speaks very favourably of Eva Smith and their breakup, saying,

> "She was - very gallant - about it"

We can draw a juxtaposition between Sheila and Eva Smith because both are young females and both products of Edwardian Society. However, there is a dramatic contrast between the two ladies as Priestley very skilfully portrays their character. Eva Smith being the victim and Sheila the privileged, socialite.

Priestley allows for their lives to become intertwined, and he very bitterly unfold for us how Sheila, being the social elite of the Edwardian capitalist class abused her power to turn Eva Smith's world upside down.

By having her fired she set off a chain of events, hence causing a ripple effect which ultimately contributed to her death although later in the play, she was very remorseful for her actions.

The Inspector deliberately described her death with a visual graphic picture,

"burnt inside out"

so that the Birling's can actually visualise the scene and take stock of their actions. Priestley wants the inspector to target their conscience and he was desperate for the ignorant, privileged, Capitalist class to become more socially mobile and responsible for the poor Socialist class and their woes.

The Inspector makes constant reference to Eva Smith's suffering and desperation, detailing how she became 'lonely and desperate'. The Birling's ruthless prejudice against her and their ignorance and arrogance led to her horrific death. The Inspector makes another emotive statement which gets the readers emotionally involved – she had no savings from the low wages she earned and that she had no parents to go back to and because of the Birlings action she slid deeper into the depths of despair, and she had to seek alternate employment.

Priestley is angered that the rich upper classes exploited the poor as Mr Birling said,

"for lower costs and higher prices."

and the rich climbed the social ladder at the expense of the poor. In his final speech the Inspector says that,

"there are millions and millions and millions of Eva Smiths"

whose lives, hopes and fears are

"intertwined with our lives"

and if we don't share collective responsibility and empathy towards their suffering then, the Inspector warns, we will be taught in
"fire and blood and anguish"
And will hence incur the wrath of God.

SOCIAL RESPONSIBILITY

One may argue that the play 'An Inspector Calls' focuses more on themes, and social issues rather than driven by plot. Priestley writes very passionately to reinforce his socialist message and the damaging aristocratic Capitalist message of the Edwardian era. He employs various dramatic techniques and strategies like tension, suspense, conflict, entrances and exits, beginnings and ends, and linguistic devices to pioneer a new morality in politics. He uses these as a vehicle to convey his ideas about social responsibility. Most of the characters have a very skewed and narrow view of the theme of responsibility. Mr Birling – a careful construct of the Aristocratic Capitalist of the Edwardian society – is portrayed as an avaricious, pompous, and ignorant businessman. He describes himself as

"a hard-headed businessman," who we see, only cares about making profit.

and making sure that

"our interests and the interest of capital are properly protected"

His capitalist, selfish message of

"a man has to make his own way and take care of himself and his family"

is conveyed to Gerald and Eric, and at this opportune moment the doorbell rings and the Inspector enters creating a conflict of ideas between the Inspector and Mr Birling. He also uses animal imagery,

"being mixed together like bees in a hive"

to reinforce his distaste for Socialist ideals. There is a stark contrast between the Capitalist belief of Mr Birling and the Socialist belief of the Inspector. Priestley uses the Inspector to bring about social changes in the Edwardian Pre-World War One era. Priestley uses dramatic irony to highlight Mr Birling's beliefs, said with such confidence and conviction that the Titanic will not sink and that World War One will not happen, which proved to be wrong. Priestley deliberately creates a negative impression of Mr Birling and his ignorance to intensify his distaste for the Capitalist social climbers like Mr Birling who refuse to accept responsibility. Hence, Priestley tries to convey a message of social mobility and responsibility through his God – like, construct – The Inspector, who is authoritative, level-headed, and not threatened by the social status of the Birlings. He uses harsh and blunt questioning techniques and force the Birlings to admit to their role in Eva Smith's death. However, Mr Birling refused to accept responsibility, describing it as

"awkward to have to accept responsibility for everything that happens to everybody."

The character of Mrs Birling, carefully moulded by Priestley to portray her as an obnoxious, self-indulgent, egotistical product of the aristocrat Capitalist class.

"A rather cold woman"

clearly depicts Priestley's dislike of her. Mrs Birling is a social snob and firmly believes that her responsibility is to arbiter and ensure the appropriate behaviour patterns of her family and public morality. Her prejudices about behaviour when she insists that the father of Eva Smith's child should be publicly scorned, and that the girl had herself to blame and believed that Eva Smith was not deserving of help. Yet she had a very misguided view that her responsibility is to the poor who deserve it. Ironically, Gerald displayed a collective responsibility when he rescued Eva Smith, yet he went on to commit the offence he saved her from. He was cut from the same cloth as the Birlings and refused to accept responsibility and never changed at the end of the play and continued their lives as before.

Sheila is the most willing to fully accept her responsibility for her actions. She showed genuine remorse and was prepared to atone for the error of her ways. Eric too acted in quite a responsible way when he does accept responsibility for Eva Smith's pregnancy and although he stole money and gave her, he did not totally abandon her. Sadly, although goaded by the Inspector not everyone was prepared to accept personal responsibility in Eva Smith's death. Priestley exposes the prejudices of class, wealth, power, and greed can have on the stance taken in relation to responsibility.

Sheila and Eric – the younger generation was Priestley's vision for the future. He wanted the younger generation to become socially mobile and hoped that they will bring about social changes for the proletariats. He yearned for societal shifts for change and used them as a vehicle to pioneer equality and better working conditions and to break down the barriers that existed between the avaricious Capitalist Class and the poor socialist class. The words responsible and responsibility are used by most characters in the play. The Inspector wants everyone to share responsibility in Eva Smith's death and tells them bluntly,

"each of you helped to kill her"
He is talking of collective responsibility.
"There are millions and millions and millions of Eva Smiths"
The Inspector, says that
"everyone is part of one body"
He is propounding Priestley's socialist views who wanted the characters to develop a social conscience and to embrace a collective responsibility. He warns them that if they ignore their responsibility then they will be,
"taught it in fire and blood and anguish."
If injustice and inequality persist then they will be answerable to God. He uses a missionary tone and vociferously thunders out Priestley's political message and the Inspector and the Inspector's prophetic, oratorical style confirms his omniscience, God-like status.

Priestley was passionate to express his controversial politically charged messages of Socialism. Priestley draws a sharp contrast between the generations, and he tries to pioneer a new morality in politics,

"We are members of one body, we are responsible for each other"

The theme of responsibility is a fine thread running throughout the play screaming out Priestley's message of Social Responsibility. The younger generation, Eric and Sheila was Priestley' vision for the future.

He portrays them in a very favourable light because there are glaring changes in their behaviour as the play progresses. Priestley firmly believes that they will be a catalyst for change. Their acceptance of their responsibility for their actions can be starkly contrasted to that of their parents who refused to accept responsibility,

"I accept no blame for it at all"

was Mrs Birling's response to Eva Smith's death.

"I was perfectly justified"

The ignorance and avaricious nature of the Birling's is juxtaposed to the understanding and experience of the younger generation. Sheila's response to Old Joe Meggarty's behaviour can be contrasted to that of Mrs Birling's reaction.

In Act 2 Gerald explains how he met Eva Smith and he proceeds to explain how

"Old Joe Meggarty's, half drunk and goggle-eyed"

accosted Eva Smith. Mrs Birling's shock response is depicted by the use of the rhetorical question,

"Surely you don't' mean Alderman Meggarty?"

Her capitalist beliefs make her deny that he is capable of such vile behaviour because he is the upstanding pillar of society. Priestley mocks the Capitalist Class for having 'skeletons in their cupboards' and their superficial way of life angers him.

He writes with disdain about the hypocrisy of the rich aristocratic class who only pretend to be respectable. Sheila very promptly adds credence to the embarrassing situation by declaring, but everybody knows about that 'horrible Meggarty'.

Mrs Birling adds a very sanctimonious title to Meggarty, 'Alderman'. It is evident here how Mrs Birling sees her capitalist world through 'rose tinted' glasses. Sheila adds fuel to the fire by creating a visual picture about how a girl escaped from Meggarty with a torn blouse. Priestley clearly illustrates the generational differences between the women's idea of depravity and corruption, in men of superior status.

Mr Birling is the perfect caricature of capitalism. He is a staunch capitalist who refused to accept responsibility for his actions. There is a huge generational clash of ideas between Eric and his father. There is a great distance between the two and Eric has a sense of insecurity and feels that he cannot go to his father for help. He becomes stronger as the play progresses and he develops into a catalyst for social change. Eric is angry when he learns that his father fired Eva Smith,

"Why shouldn't they try for higher wages"

Mr Birling becomes furious with Eric and warns him,

"It's about time you learnt to face some responsibilities"

When Mrs Birling walks in briskly and dismisses the Inspector's questioning as 'absurd' Sheila urges her mother to listen to the Inspector and not to

"build a wall"

because the Inspector will break it down.

Mrs Birling becomes angry with Sheila for contradicting her. Here it is clearly evident that Sheila is more perceptive than her mother. Once again Priestley highlights his faith in the younger generation and his distaste for the morals and ideals of the older generation. There were different reactions between the generations when the workers went on strike at the Birling's factory. Mr Birling was very cold in his response,

"She had to go"

And Sheila's emotive response was,

"but these girls aren't cheap labour – they're people"

The stark contrast between the two generations is that the younger generation took responsibility and learnt many lessons from the Inspector, whereas the older generation refused to take responsibility for their action. Mr and Mrs Birling were bent on nursing their egos and their reputation. Mrs Birling also remarks that the Inspector has had a huge impact on the younger generation and remarked that the Inspector had made a great impression on Sheila. Although Mrs Birling is portrayed to be a model aristocratic Capitalist female with all the trappings of the rich, we can detect an absence of understanding, love and compassion. She is totally out of touch with the younger generation which is clearly visible when we witness the various clashes between them.

Eric was furious with her, and he accused her of killing Eva Smith and her own grandchild. He almost comes to blows with his mother and a horrified Mr Birling intervenes. He is furious and calls Eric a 'fool' and almost gets physical with him. We see Mr Birlings coldness and a certain detachment towards Eric. Furthermore, he sided with Mrs Birling. The audience is left speechless after the Inspector leaves because the Birling's resumed their normal lives. Even Gerald told Sheila that everything was okay and gives her the ring back which she refuses.

The reaction of the younger generation like Sheila and Eric warms the audience towards them. They were shocked at their parent's behaviour and accused them of pretending that nothing happened, and everything is back to normal. Sheila tells them that they are,

"ready to go on in the same old way"

Both Eric and Sheila said that,

"It frightens me the way you talk and I can't listen to any more of it"

At the end of the play, we see that the Inspector has successfully passed on Priestley's message of social and collective responsibility, and he used Sheila and Eric to be catalysts to enforce this message and help to eradicate the exploitation of the poor. Priestley's poignant message was to encourage societal shifts towards a fairer, equal, Edwardian society of pre – World War One.

Edwardian Britain saw a huge divide between the aristocratic Capitalist class and the poor Socialist working class. Priestley viewed with deep concern how the bulk of the country's wealth was enjoyed by a few people like the rich factory owners and the Birling's and the Croft's are classic examples of the avaricious Capitalist class of Edwardian Britain.

In 1912 these selfish aristocrats were very comfortable with their positions and didn't want to change the status quo. Therefore, Priestley fought, using the Inspector as a catalyst to convey his message of social mobility and equality and justice for all.

The underlying themes of power and class are dominating themes which sets the wheels in motion in, 'An Inspector Calls'. The rigid class system in the Edwardian Era which saw the rise of Mr Birling, who from a modest background had made his way up the social ladder, hence becoming Mayor of Brumley, serving as a magistrate and his impending knighthood.

He is described as being 'rather provincial' in his speech,' Priestley is hinting that he does not speak proper standard English like that of an aristocrat because he is 'new money' unlike his wife who is his 'social superior.' In the Edwardian era the rich Capitalist class wielded much power over the poor Socialist class as is evident in the shoddy treatment of Eva Smith.

Each of the characters had in some way abused their social status and power in destroying Eva Smith which ultimately led to her death. Mr Birling's desire to move up the social ladder almost borders on comic. This need is so glaring that he tells Gerald,
    "You are just the kind of son-in-law I always wanted"
He very pompously declares with the utmost pride that the Crofts and the Birlings will work together
    "for lower costs and higher prices"
Priestley writes with a bitter tone here to emphasise the fact that their ill-gotten gains are due to the exploitation of the poor Socialist class. Mrs Birling is the epitome of social snobbery. She places great emphasis on prioritising social status and decorum. She stems from the typical aristocratic Edwardian female, all powerful and confident with an air of superiority about her. She is intolerant of those who she perceives to be of inferior social status to her.

This is quite evident in her shabby treatment of Eva Smith and her persistent use of euphemisms,
    "girl of that sort"
exposes her hypocrisy.

Living in her socially elite cocoon she was unable to grasp the realities of the sufferings and needs of those less fortunate than her. She firmly believed that women from the poorer social class had no morals and wouldn't dare to refuse money. Priestley creates a morality play and he shows his dissatisfaction to the Birling's superficial existence which displayed no true sense of morality because they treated Eva Smith appallingly and contributed to her sad demise.

HOW DOES PRIESTLEY PRESENT THE INSPECTOR ?

'An Inspector Calls' was set in 1912, only 2 years before WW1, however it was written in 1954 by J.B. Priestley. Priestley writes this play to teach people about social responsibility.

In the play, Eva Smith alias Daisy Renton – the tragic victim exploited by the Birlings and Gerald Croft but whose story was resurrected by Inspector Goole to make the exploiters face up to their guilt. The Inspector is the advocate for Eva Smith! J.B. Priestley presents the Inspector in many ways to make the audience wonder who he really is. Firstly, Priestley presents the Inspector as a mysterious character who slowly, smoothly, and sensibly unravels the mystery behind the tragic death of Eva Smith.

In Act One, Birling said to the Inspector, "You're new, aren't you?" The Inspector is omniscient but does not reveal too much about himself. When he leaves the house, he leaves the Birlings and the audience wondering who he actually was. Another mystery is the way the Inspector comes and leaves the house. Priestley presents the Inspector in this way to show the Birlings and Gerald as well as audience that we each have to take responsibility for each other. This responsibility would be needed for Britain to survive the forthcoming World War. People had to work together and be together in harmony. They had to care about the poor and not class people, such as working, middle and higher classes. Everyone should be treated the same.

The Inspector is presented as an unbiased, fair character by Priestley. In Act Three, the Inspector said to Sheila, "You helped – but didn't start it." Sheila Birling had learnt her lesson; therefore, the Inspector does not pick on her. However, Mr Arthur Birling had not, and the Inspector vents his anger – (*rather savagely, to Birling*) "You started it." followed by "And now she'll (*Eva Smith*) make you pay a heavier price still." The Inspector concludes by saying, "One Eva Smith has gone – but there are millions of Eva Smiths" and "if men will not learn that lesson, then they will be taught it in fire and blood and anguish", before walking out, leaving the Birlings and Gerald staring, subdued and wondering! Priestley is instructing the audience through the verbal interactions of the Inspector and the Birlings about the importance of social responsibility.

Priestley presents the Inspector as a seriously hard-working character whose duty is to teach the Birlings and Gerald about social responsibility. This is shown when the Inspector arrives half-way through Act One. Arthur Birling said, "Have a glass of port – or a little whisky?" Priestley presents the Inspector as a seriously hard-working character whose duty is to teach the Birlings and Gerald about social responsibility. This is shown when the Inspector arrives half-way through Act One. Arthur Birling said, "Have a glass of port – or a little whisky?"

The Inspector rebuffs this by saying, "No, thank you, Mr Birling. I'm on duty." The Inspector is not at the Birlings' house to socialise but to do his duty and only his duty. The Inspector is there to teach the Birlings and Gerald about the essence of social responsibility by uncovering the consequences that led to the calamitous death of Eva Smith. Priestley uses the Inspector as a hammer to crack a nut as under conditions of class, the Birlings would not take the death of an underprivileged person like Eva Smith seriously, simply because the Birlings and Gerald considered themselves to belong to a superior class.

Priestley presents the Inspector as an advocate of truth and justice, who is not afraid to engage and chastise the higher echelons of society. As seen in Act Two, when Mrs Sybil Birling said (*to Inspector, rather grandly*) "I realise that you may have to conduct some sort of inquiry, but I must say that so far you seem to be conducting it in a rather peculiar and offensive manner." The Inspector is not phased by this outburst but moves on to interrogate the next guilty person on his list, Mr Birling who according to Mrs Birling will be back shortly. The Inspector is following his strategy of pursuing one line of enquiry at a time so that there is no collusion between the guilty parties – the truth must be discovered by each guilty person in the play. Priestley is educating the audience in the consequences of not understanding social responsibility. Through the actions of the Inspector, Priestley is inciting the reader to stand up and be brave, to fight for their rights. Everyone must treat everyone else both fairly and equally!

Priestley presents the Inspector as a character that symbolises events. In Act One, the scene setting describes the Inspector as, '*a man in his fifties, dressed in a plain darkish suit of the period.*' This signifies the horrific death of Eva Smith by committing suicide by drinking disinfectant. In 1912, people wore dark clothes to funerals, a tradition still prevalent in today's society. The Inspector's attire is deliberate to enforce and to remind those responsible of the seriousness of their previous actions leading to the death of Eva Smith alias Daisy Renton.

Priestley also presents the Inspector as a controlling character who manipulates the Birlings and Gerald to see and accept the errors of their ways – social responsibility cannot be ignored. Right from the start, Priestley introduces the Inspector as not a '*big man*' but a man who '*creates at once an impression of massiveness, solidity and purposefulness*'. From then on, the Inspector is in charge, deciding who to interview and when not phased by protests from Mrs Birling or Mr Birling. In Act Two, Mrs Birling berates the Inspector by saying to the Inspector, "I must say that so far you seem to be conducting it in a rather peculiar and offensive manner" and later in Act Two, Mr Birling said, "Is there any reason why my wife should answer questions from you, Inspector?" By Act Three, the Inspector has got Mr Birling and Mrs Birling's attention as to the seriousness of their actions together with those of Sheila, Eric, and Gerald in the demise of Eva Smith.

The Inspector is totally in control of events, and once convinced that all the guilty parties had understood their roles departs from the house leaving them *'staring, subdued and wondering.'* In effect, Priestley controls the moral message of social responsibility through the character and actions of the Inspector.

Priestley also presents the Inspector as a person who makes the guilty parties realise each other's mistakes. This is shown by the conflict he causes between the guilty parties after the Inspector had left. Near the end of Act Three, immediately after the Inspector departed, Mr Birling said (*angrily to Eric*) "You're the one I blame for this." The Inspector had fragmented the guilty parties.

Before the Inspector arrived midway in Act One, there was order and hierarchy with Mr Arthur Birling in charge supported by his wife Mrs Sybil Birling. By midway in Act Three, the guilty parties had split into those such as Sheila, Eric and Gerald who had understood their roles in the demise of Eva Smith and those such as Arthur Birling and Sybil Birling who still clung to their prejudices and considered themselves free of responsibility – absolved. This shows that in reality the Birlings and Gerald were not a stable unit despite initial impressions painted by Priestley at the start of the play. The Inspector like ice and fire, cracked their solidity by careful manipulation of each of the guilty parties getting Sheila, Eric, and Gerald to change their mindset. However, some mindsets cannot be changed. He clearly failed with the older generation represented by Arthur and Sybil.

Priestley presents the Inspector as an unidentified character. In Act Two, the Inspector replied to Mrs Birling by saying, (*gravely*) "We'll see, Mrs Birling." This tells us that the Inspector is in no mood to let others like Mrs Birling dictate the pace or direction of the interrogation. Hence the stage direction for the Inspector to act *'gravely'*. In Act Three, Mrs Birling reacting to Mr Birling's phone call to Colonel Roberts that no Inspector Goole existed, says "I felt it all the time. He never talked like one. He never looked like one". Again, Sheila in response to Eric, said "He never seemed like an ordinary police inspector- Both dialogues support Priestley's representation of the Inspector as an omniscient character. Apart from the dialogue, Priestley further cements the Inspector as an omniscient character by phonetics – by giving the Inspector the name 'Goole' which sounds very similar to 'Ghoul'. The connotation makes the Inspector eerie and a threat to the other participates in the play. The audience's expectations are piqued by this clever phonetic device.

Finally, Priestley presents the Inspector as a God like character. Suddenly, out of the blue, the phone rings, and Mr Birling learns that a girl has just died on her way to the infirmary after swallowing dome disinfectant, and a police inspector is on his way to ask some questions. What Inspector Goole has told them is coming true but this time it will be a real inspector who will quiz them – only an omniscient, God-like character could have predicted the event before it happened!

JB Priestley uses 'An Inspector Calls' to express controversial, politically charged messages of social reforms. Priestley tries to pioneer a new morality in politics. One of the main themes of the play is social responsibility. "We are members of one body. We are responsible for each other." This extract is taken from the Inspector's last speech before departing from the house, and I think that it sums up exactly what Priestley was trying to get across about social responsibility. He uses a range of linguistic devices in order to intensify his message.

"Birling is a heavy looking, rather portentous man in his mid fifties", this quote denotes that he is a self-centred, callous man who is also used as a parody for the audience's amusement. "Hard headed business man" is what he describes himself as, which is exactly how the audience sees him. Mrs Birling is portrayed as a cold arrogant woman. She seems to bring in a negative tone and atmosphere when she speaks. Both Mr and Mrs Birling show ostentatious mannerisms which emphasises their good fortune.

On the other hand, Eric and Sheila are amiable and considerate. Priestley describes Sheila as a 'very pretty girl in her early twenties, very pleased with life and rather excited'. She thus starts to play as someone whom the audience would regard as superficial however, this changes once she hears about the death of Eva and her part in it and she becomes more sensitive and caring. On the contrary, Gerald who is now engaged to Sheila is very self-confident and at ease with anyone he comes into contact with, which are his main traits. He is very courteous and tactful towards the Birlings, "I insist upon being part of the family".

The Inspector is used as the voice of the ordinary people's conscience. The Inspector exhibits the ordinary people's views on society. The Birlings hear the sharp ring of a door bell, the portent to symbolism and dramatic irony to come. The audience is aware that it is the Inspector at the door, but the Birlings and Gerald do not. The lighting turns from 'pink and intimate' which is comforting to 'hard and bright' putting the Birlings and Gerald under the spotlight. This change in lighting foreshadows the events about to come – it indicates it will not be pleasant or happy. This change also denotes the power and importance of the Inspector. The Inspector connects with each character in the dining room – psychologically pressuring them to open up and take responsibility and blame.

Priestley deliberately makes the Inspector use powerful adjectives in his phrases such as 'burnt her inside out' and 'she was in great agony' to target the compassionate side of the other characters. This also creates a distressing image of Eva in the audience's minds. Mr Birling is the first to be interviewed and interrogated and admits to firing Eva but refuses to accept any responsibility or blame for her death. Mr Birling takes offence and counters by saying, (*staring at the Inspector*) "What did you say your name was, Inspector?", followed by "How do you get on with our Chief constable", and then, "Perhaps I ought to warn you that he's an old friend of mine". This does not deter the Inspector continuing with and pursuing his line of questioning. The Inspector is in charge not Mr Birling!

Within the play, both Mr Birling and the Inspector Goole clash over who is to blame. Their philosophies are diamagnetic, the Inspector places the blame on the Birlings and Gerald, winning over Sheila, Eric, and Gerald to accepting their responsibility for Eva's death, but failing miserably to convince Mr Birling and his wife of their part in the tragedy.

In Act One, before the Inspector arrives on the scene, Mr Birling's views and philosophies are expounded to Gerald and the audience, typified by "a man has to make his own way – has to look after himself – and his family too." Social responsibility and blame is not an issue as far as Mr Birling and the older generation are concerned. The sharp ring of change happens when the Inspector arrives to dispel the idea that no one person is to blame. Mr and Mrs Birling are in for a pounding!

Sheila acknowledges she used her power to 'punish' Eva Smith. She regrets her actions. Consequently, she now feels empathy towards Eva, as does Eric. She accepts that she contributed to Eva's demise by saying, "I went to the manager at Milwards and told him that if they didn't get rid of that girl, I'd never go near the place again and I'd persuade mother to close our account with them." The reason for her actions was jealousy and being in a bad temper.

Unlike Sheila, Gerald is not as willing to admit any wrong doing on his part in the affair of Eva's death, initially pretending not to have known Eva. But eventually accepts that he left Eva homeless and alone. Having revealed everything to the Inspector and everyone else, Gerald reveals his true emotions when he asks the Inspector, "In that case – as I'm rather more – upset – by this business than I probably appear to be – and – well, I'd like to be alone for a while – I'd be glad if you'd let me go." Although sad for what happened to Eva, Gerald finds it difficult to accept blame when his only motive was to help Eva in some way, even though he exploited her like many affluent men seeking pleasure did, in the Edwardian era.

Mrs Birling is unsympathetic and seems to shy from away from any reality which is not part of her social upper class. She persistently refuses to accept any responsibility or blame for the death of Eva Smith alias Daisy Renton.

She tells the Inspector, "I'm sorry she should have come to such a horrible end. But I accept no blame for it at all." As chairwomen of the Brumley Women's Charity Organisation, Mrs Birling's instructions to Eva when she came before the committee was to, "Go and look for the father of the child. It's his responsibility." The irony is that later as the Inspector questions Eric, it dawns on Mrs Birling that the father of the child was, in fact, Eric her own son. Despite Sheila's interventions to convince Mother of the Birling's complicity in the death of Eva Smith, Mrs Birling is still unrepentant, still stuck in the old social beliefs that the upper class is not to blame for, or responsible for, those below her class who should follow Mr Birling's example by bettering themselves by their own industries.

Eric is remorseful about his behaviour towards Eva Smith who he learnt from the Inspector had been abandoned by Gerald. His behaviour in getting Eva pregnant while drunk; in manipulating Eva to taking him into her lodgings because she felt he was "in that state when a chap easily turns nasty." This led to Eric stealing money from the office to the dismay of Eva who refused to take stolen money. The Inspector informs Eric that Eva then went to his mother's committee for help but was refused any help. Nearly at breaking point, Eric directs his frustrations and emotions towards his mother saying, "Then – you killed her – my child – your own grandchild – damn you". Later, with the Inspector gone, in reaction to Mr Birlings concerns about "a downright public scandal", Eric vents his contempt by shouting, "And I say the girl's dead and we all helped to kill her – and that's what matter –". As far as Eric is concerned, all the participants in Eva's demise are to blame!

The Inspector's final departing words to the Birlings and Gerald are, "One Eva Smith has gone - but there are millions and millions and millions of Eva Smiths . . ." followed by, "all intertwined with our lives" and then "We are responsible for each other." The blame is with society and its artificial and dysfunctional divisions: poor, middle and upper classes. Priestley gets the Inspector to issue a biblical warning, "if men will not learn that lesson, then they will be taught it in fire and blood and anguish." The message Priestley is keen to get across is that social responsibility mitigates blame.

In conclusion, Priestley recognises that the older generation are set in their ways and are unlikely to change their social attitudes to blame. The younger generation, however, are different, better educated with less attachment to the old barriers defined by social class. Sheila and Eric accept and acknowledge their part in Eva Smith's downfall – Arthur, Sybil and Gerald do not!

HOW DOES PRIESTLEY EXPLORE AND DEVELOP THE BIRLING FAMILY ?

Priestley uses 'An Inspector Calls' to express his opinion on life in the early twentieth century and to show his socialist views and the attack of capitalism. The book was written in 1946 after the Second War World but set in 1912 before the First World War. This is because Priestley wanted to use dramatic irony throughout the play so that the audience could know a chain of events before the characters, one example of this is the quote about the Titanic and how it was 'unsinkable' like Capitalism. Priestley was a socialist and believed that capitalists had the wrong attitude in life, which is portrayed to the audience very early on in the play. Due to the fact that Priestley had lived through both wars he used a common problem of social responsibilities in the play. This includes the upper class getting richer and more powerful and the lower class getting poorer and weaker. Priestley also expresses his thoughts and feelings by using the Inspector in the play as his mouthpiece in order to voice his opinions.

From the outset Priestley portrays the Birling's home as a cold and unwelcoming place. The home symbolises the Birlings, cold and unwelcoming except to those belonging to people of their class. Priestley is projecting his view of society and the upper class, and, in particular, the alienation of those outside that class. Priestley reinforces his view with lighting imagery. Before the Inspector arrives, the Birlings are illuminated by 'pink and intimate' lighting. This suddenly changes to 'brighter and harder' lighting on arrival of the Inspector. The change in lighting signals a change in mood and tone. A clash from comfort to accountability as the merriment of the engagement party transforms into interrogation over the tragic life and death of Eva Smith alias Daisy Renton (and later) alias Mrs Birling.

Priestley portrays Arthur Birling as supreme head of the Birling family and as a selfish business man who thinks that the world evolves around him and that "a man has to mind his own business and look after himself and his own." Priestley develops the character of Arthur Birling by making his appearance in tune with that expected by the audience for an upperclass business man – 'a heavy looking portentous man in his fifties' – a figure unworthy to represent society whose wealth and position achieved on the backs of the workers, the lower classes.

The description of Arthur also gives the impression that he is self-centred, heartless and someone with a threatening appearance. Priestley further develops the character of Arthur by use the of alliteration when he describes Arthur as a 'Hard Headed' business man. Priestley also uses animal imagery to reveal the attitude of Arthur Birling to others. The quote "like bees in a hive" reveals Arthur's selfish mind. The simile is used by Arthur to describe socialist behaviour which he is against saying "you'd think everybody has to look after everybody else."

The demise and death of Eva Smith is dismissed by Mr Birling as not his responsibility even though, just before the Inspector departs in Act Three, the Inspector said to Birling (*rather savagely*) "You started it.", referring to Mr Birling's firing of Eva from his factory. Only then does Mr Birling try to mitigate his guilt by saying (*unhappily*) "Look, Inspector – I'd give thousands – yes, thousands –." The Inspector rejects the offer by saying "You're offering the money at the wrong time Mr Birling." Priestley is making the point that people from Mr Birling's class think that in the last resort, payment of money removes guilt like paying a religious penitence to absolve sin.

Mr Birling's mindset that his life is about business, progress and "the interests of capital." He is adamant that "we're in for a time of steadily increasing prosperity." Nowhere does he talk about how those less privileged than himself can benefit or progress. Priestley is subtly, deliberately, and sublimely making the audience question whether society is properly in balance when one part of society is ignored.

Priestley endows Mr Birling with an unassailable persona of doggedness. "Look at the progress we're making – Titanic – unsinkable, absolutely unsinkable." The repetition of the word 'unsinkable' reveals his misplaced confidence and excessive pride. The connection is that like the Titanic, Mr Birling and his family and friends are 'unsinkable'. But like the Iceberg which will sink the 'unsinkable' Titanic in a few days' time, Inspector Goole will do the same to Mr Birling and his family and soon to be brother-in-law Gerald Croft. Priestley has introduced dramatic irony because Mr Birling's prediction of the 'unsinkable' Titanic turns out to be false as does his expectations of being on the next Honours list for a knighthood.

Sheila Birling is described by Priestley as 'girl very pleased with life and rather excited'. Priestley juxtaposes her character to that of Mr Birling. Sheila is from the younger generation with a more inclusive attitude and mindset to society unlike Mr Birling from the older generation where hierarchy and social position dictate living standards.

Before the Inspector arrives, Sheila is happy and content, celebrating her engagement to Gerald Croft at dinner with other members of the Birling family. Interacting with her brother Eric in a playful way, saying "You are squiffy"

After the Inspector arrives, Sheila becomes exposed to the harsh realities of the underprivileged, deprived world of Eva Smith, a victim of prejudice and neglect. At first, Sheila is horrified at Eva's demise and death, "Oh – how horrible! Was it an accident?" Still unsure, and not knowing that she was involved, Sheila learns that Eva was fired by Mr Birling but gained employment at Milwards, a department store frequented by the Birling family. Still confused as to why the Inspector should be questioning the Birling family and why the family should take responsibility for Eva's death, "You talk as if we were responsible-", Sheila is shocked when the Inspector shows her a photograph of Eva, 'She looks at it closely, recognises it with a little cry, and then runs out'.

Sheila returns and the Inspector skilfully extracts from her the reason why she coerced the store into firing Eva. Apparently, Sheila said, "Because I was in a furious temper", and then agreed with the Inspector when he said, "you might be said to have been jealous of her." Now, Sheila realises her contribution to Eva's demise and death. Now, Sheila is repentant and wishes to make amends in some way, "if I could help her now, I would." Now, Sheila knows that the Inspector is omniscient, and other family members will soon be drawn into the tragedy. At the end of Act One, in reply to Gerald, Sheila (*laughs rather hysterically*) "Why – you fool – he knows" followed by "And I hate to think how much he knows that we don't know yet."

Throughout Acts Two and Three, Sheila's attitude is transformed by supporting the Inspector's actions to get others in the family to accept responsibility for their part in Eva's death, "Well, he inspected us all right. And don't let's start dodging and pretending now." Between us we drove that girl to commit suicide.

Priestley deliberately uses the character of Sheila as a catalyst for change. Sheila is the vehicle that in a biblical sense preaches to the non-believers and sinners – the older generation maybe beyond redemption, but the younger generation can be saved because they are more compassionate and willing to change.

Mrs Birling is described by Priestley as 'a cold arrogant woman'. She is self-centred and a dutiful wife to Mr Birling. She has her own social standing and chairs the Brumley Women's Charity Organisation, an organisation to which women in distress can appeal for help in various forms. She is delighted that Sheila her daughter, is engaged to Gerald, son of Sir George Croft who owns a friendly, larger rival company to the Birlings, but outside her social circle, she is a snob with no real concern for the under-privileged.

Priestley is rigid with this character Mrs Sybil Birling. There is no real change in her character even when dragged through the process of her involvement in the demise of Eva Smith.

Priestley presents both Sybil and Arthur Birling as part of the older generation, blinkered in their outlook and dogmatic in their views and actions. Mr Birling says to Gerald, "I have an idea that your mother - Lady Croft – while she doesn't object to my girl – feels you might have done better for yourself socially." Mrs Birling in reply to the Inspector, "And in spite of what's happened to the girl (*Eva*) since, I consider I did my duty."

Priestley uses Eric as a lever to prize open the capitalist insensitivity to human suffering, berating both his parents, Arthur, and Sybil, for their lack of compassion. Although responsible for Eva's pregnancy whilst in a drunken condition, and the subsequent theft of money to support her, Eric redeems himself by accepting responsibility for his past actions in the demise of Eva Smith, and by challenging his parent's dismissive rhetoric over the issue. Eric to his parents, "What's the use of talking about behaving sensibly. You're beginning to pretend now that nothing's really happened at all. This girl's still dead, isn't she?"

As the play progresses, Priestley develops Eric's character from an immature, non-thinking, womanising capitalist indoctrinated youth with a drink addiction, to a thoughtful, remorseful, compassionate champion of the socialist values and beliefs.

In conclusion, Priestley is inviting the audience to question the practices of society be it in 1912 when the play was set or in 1946 when in production. He uses the Birling family as a vehicle to explore the ethical and wealth issues which divide a nation. By the end of the play, Eric and Sheila are converted to the ideas of socialism, whereas Arthur Birling and his wife Sybil Birling, remain firm, rejecting any wrong doing in the Eva Smith affair. Gerald Croft sits on the fence, to become part of the Birling family, convinced that his motives towards Eva Smith were genuine and therefore free of guilt.

1. How does Priestley's portrayal of Gerald Croft contribute to the dramatic impact of the play?
2. How does Priestley use stage directions in An Inspector Calls?
3. How does the relationship between Sheila and Gerald develop?
4. Write about Inspector Goole's role in the play. How far is he a believable policeman?
5. How does Priestley make the Inspector's presence on the stage powerful and dominating?
6. "We don't live alone. We are members of one body. We are responsible for each other." Discuss the theme of social responsibility.
7. Explore how Priestley presents a class-ridden, hypocritical society.
8. Although Eva Smith does not appear on stage, she plays a major role in the play. To what extent do you agree?
9. How does Sheila develop throughout the play?
10. The play is full of lies and deceit. Explain how Priestley exposes weakness and wickedness in characters and society?
11. The Inspector's inquiry makes the Birlings quarrel among themselves. How does Priestley develop the internal conflicts in the play?
12. How does Priestley create suspense and mystery in An Inspector Calls?
13. How does Priestley explore the ideas of socialism in the play?
14. How does Priestley present the character of Mrs Birling in the play?
15. How does Priestley present the character of Eric in the play?
16. How does Priestley explore the ideas of status and power in the play?
17. How does Priestley present the theme of poverty in the play?
18. How and why does Eric change in the play?
19. How does Priestley present the theme of blame in the play?
20. How does Priestley explore the issue of class in An Inspector Calls?
21. How far does Priestley present Mr Birling as an unlikeable character in the play?
22. How does Priestley explore the theme of morality in An Inspector Calls?
23. Sheila and Eric are said to be Priestley's vision for the future. Discuss the theme of generation gap.
24. Discuss the difference between the characters of Eric and Gerald?
25. Discuss the theme of socialism.
26. "An Inspector Calls is patronising and overly moralising. We don't need theatre to teach us how to behave." To what extent do you agree?
27. How does Priestley present different ideas about power and influence in An Inspector Calls?
28. How does Priestley present ideas about unfairness in society in An Inspector Calls?
29. How does Priestley present ideas about attitudes towards women in An Inspector Calls?
30. How does Priestley use the character of Mr Birling to communicate his political views?
31. At the beginning of the play, Birling says: "the way some of these cranks talk and write now, you'd think everybody has to look after everybody else, as if we were all mixed up together like bees in a hive." What is the significance of this statement?

1 | 1 How far does Priestley present Eric as a character who changes his attitudes towards himself and others during the play?
Write about:
- what Eric says and does throughout the play
- how far Priestley presents Eric as a character who changes his attitudes.

1 | 2 How does Priestley explore the importance of social class
in *An Inspector Calls?*
Write about:
- some ideas about social class in the play
- how Priestley presents the importance of social class.

2 | 1 How does Priestley present selfishness and its effects in *An Inspector Calls?*

Write about:
- examples of selfish behaviour in the play
- how Priestley presents selfishness and its effects.

2 | 2 How does Priestley explore the importance of Shiela's character
in An Inspector Calls?
Write about:
- some of the things Sheila learns in the play
- how Priestley presents Sheila as a character who learns important lessons about herself and society.

3 | 1 How far does Priestley present Mrs Birling as an unlikeable character?
Write about:
- what Mrs Birling says and does in the play
- how Priestley presents her by the ways he writes.

3 | 2 How does Priestley use the character of the Inspector to suggest
ways that society could be improved?
Write about:
- what society is shown to be like in the play and how it might be improved
- how Priestley presents society through what the Inspector says and does.

4 1 Explore Priestley's portrayal of the older generation in the play.

4 2 Inspector Goole: "And I tell you that the time will soon come when,
if men will not learn that lesson, then they will be taught it
in fire and blood and anguish."
How does Priestley present the importance of the future in *An Inspector Calls?*

5 1 'The mystery of the play revolves around Inspector Goole.'
How far do you agree with this view?

5 2 In what ways does Sheila Birling change as the play progresses?

6 1 Explore Priestley's portrayal of the older generation in the play.

7 1 **Eric:** *Well, she hadn't a job – and didn't feel like trying again for one –
and she had no money left...*
Explore the significance of money in An Inspector Calls.
or

7 2 **Birling:** *I speak as a hard-headed business man, who has to take risks
and knows what he's about...*
In what ways is Mr Arthur Birling important throughout the play?

8 1 **Sheila:** *I know I'm to blame – and I'm desperately sorry... It's simply my fault.*
Explore the importance of guilty consciences in the play.
or

8 2 **Gerald:** *I'm sorry, Sheila. But it was all over and done with, last summer.
I hadn't set eyes on the girl for at least six months.*
Explore the significance of Gerald in An Inspector Calls.

9 1 What do you think of Eric and the way he is presented to an audience?
Remember to support your answer with reference to the play
and comment on its social, cultural and historical context.

9 2 Who or what is most responsible for the death of Eva Smith?
Remember to support your answer with reference to the play
and comment on its social, cultural and historical context.

Q1   **Read the Extract 1 below and then answer both part (a) and part (b).**
For **part (a)**, you should focus only on the extract here rather than referring to the rest of your studied text.
(a) Compare how conflict between parents and their siblings is presented
  - The situations and experiences faced by Sheila and Eric
  - How the siblings Sheila and Eric react to their parents
  - How language and dramatic features create effects
(b) Explore a moment earlier in the play that shows how Sheila gains a new understanding.

Extract 1 from: *An Inspector Calls* by J. B. Priestley

This scene is towards the end of the play. It now seems possible that Inspector Goole was not a real Inspector and that a girl has not died after all.

Birling: (*jovially*):
But the whole thing's different now. Come, come, you can see that, can't you?
(*Imitating Inspector in his final speech*) You all helped to kill her.
(*Pointing at Sheila and Eric, and laughing*)
And I wish you could have seen the look on your faces when he said that.
(*Sheila moves towards door.*) Going to bed, young woman?
Sheila: (*tensely*): I want to get out of this. It frightens me the way you talk.
Birling: (*heartily*): Nonsense! You'll have a good laugh over it yet. Look, you'd better ask Gerald for that ring you gave back to him hadn't you? Then you'll feel better.
Sheila: (*passionately*): You're pretending everything's just as it was before.
Eric: I'm not!
Sheila: No, but these others are.
Birling: Well, isn't it? We've been had, that's all.
Sheila: So nothing really happened. So there's nothing to be sorry for, nothing to learn. We can all go on behaving just as we did.
Mrs Birling: Well, why shouldn't we?
Sheila: I tell you – whoever that Inspector was, it was anything but a joke. You knew it then. You began to learn something. And now you've stopped. You're ready to go on in the same old way.
Birling: (amused): And you're not, eh?
Sheila: No, because I remember what he said, how he looked, and what he made me feel. Fire and blood and anguish. And it frightens me the way you talk, and I can't listen to any more of it.
Eric: I agree with Sheila. It frightens me too.
Birling: Well, go to bed then, and don't stand there being hysterical.
Mrs Birling: They're over-tired. In the morning they'll be as amused as we are.

Q2 **Read the extract below and then answer both part (a) and part (b).**
For **part (a)**, you should focus only on the extract here rather than referring to the rest of your studied text.
(a) Compare the effect of Eva Smith death as experienced by each character
- Are their sympathies the same or different
- How language and dramatic features create effects
(b) Explore another moment in *An Inspector Calls* where something shocking is revealed.

Extract from: *An Inspector Calls* by J. B. Priestley
This extract takes place moments after Sheila has re-entered the room in Act One.

Sheila: What's all this about?
Birling: Nothing to do with you, Sheila. Run along
Inspector: No, wait a minute, Miss Birling.
Birling: (*angrily*) Look here, Inspector, I consider this uncalled-for and officious. I've half a mind to report you. I've told you all I know – and it doesn't seem to me very important – and now there isn't the slightest reason why my daughter should be dragged into this unpleasant business.
Sheila: (*coming farther in*) What business? What's happening
Inspector: (*impressively*) I'm a police inspector, Miss Birling. This afternoon a young woman drank some disinfectant, and died, after several hours of agony, tonight in the Infirmary.
Sheila: Oh – how horrible! Was it an accident?
Birling: Well, don't tell me that's because I discharged her from my employment nearly two years ago.
Eric: That might have started it.

Q3   **Read the extract below. Then answer the following question:**

Look closely at how the characters speak and behave here.
How does it create mood and atmosphere for an audience?

Extract from: *An Inspector Calls* by J. B. Priestley

Mrs B.	(*smiling, social*) Good evening, Inspector
Inspector	Good evening, madam.
Mrs B.	(*same easy tone*) I'm Mrs Birling, y'know. My husband has just explained why you're here, and while we'll be glad to tell you anything you want to know, I don't think we can help you much.
Sheila	No, Mother — please!
Mrs B.	(*affecting great surprise*) What's the matter, Sheila?
Sheila	(*hesitantly*) I know it sounds silly—
Mrs B.	What does?
Sheila	You see, I feel you're beginning all wrong. And I'm afraid you'll say something or do something that you'll be sorry for afterwards
Mrs B.	I don't know what you're talking about, Sheila.
Sheila	We all started like that — so confident, so pleased with ourselves until he began asking us questions.

Mrs Birling looks from Sheila to the Inspector

Mrs B.	You seem to have made a great impression on this child, Inspector.
Inspector	(*coolly*) We often do on the young ones. They're more impressionable.

He and Mrs Birling look at each other for a moment. Then Mrs Birling turns to Sheila again.

Mrs B.	You're looking tired, dear. I think you ought to go to bed — and forget about this absurd business. You'll feel better in the morning.
Sheila	Mother, I couldn't possibly go. Nothing could be worse for me. We've settled all that. I'm staying here until I know why that girl killed herself.
Mrs B.	Nothing but morbid curiosity.
Sheila	No it isn't.
Mrs B.	Please don't contradict me like that. And in any case, I don't suppose for a moment that we can understand why the girl committed suicide. Girls of that class—
Sheila	(*urgently, cutting in*) Mother, don't — please don't. For your own sake, as well as ours, you mustn't—
Mrs B.	(*annoyed*) Mustn't – what? Really, Sheila!
Sheila	(*slowly, carefully now*) You mustn't try to build up a kind of wall between us and that girl. If you do, then the Inspector will just break it down. And it'll be all the worse when he does
Mrs B.	I don't understand you. (*To Inspector*) Do you?
Inspector	Yes. And she's right.
Mrs B.	(*haughtily*) I beg your pardon!
Inspector	(*very plainly*) I said Yes — I do understand her. And she's right.
Mrs B.	That — I consider — is a trifle impertinent, Inspector

Save

STUDY GUIDE on Priestley's AN INSPECTOR CALLS
This **GUIDE** is a **MUST** for **ALL** students to achieve **TOP** grades in English **LITERATURE**

Excellent book ★★★★★
Very clear and well written book. Gives an excellent analysis of themes and characters. Invaluable for study and gaining a clearer understanding of the text. This has been highly helpful to my son with his GCSE studies. Very highly recommended. Would rate higher if I could!

Evelyn Samuel was born in South Africa, educated at the University of Durban-Westville gaining a BA degree in English, Speech & Drama, then a Higher Education Diploma at the University of South Africa. Relocating to the UK, she acquired Qualified Teacher Status in 2006, and a Diploma in Travel Journalism in 2020. An expert in teaching English Language and Literature, Evelyn has steered many students to top grades.

Eve Super Easy Books
www.EveSuperEasyBooks.com
EveSuperEasyBooks@gmail.com

An Inspector Calls Made Super Super Easy

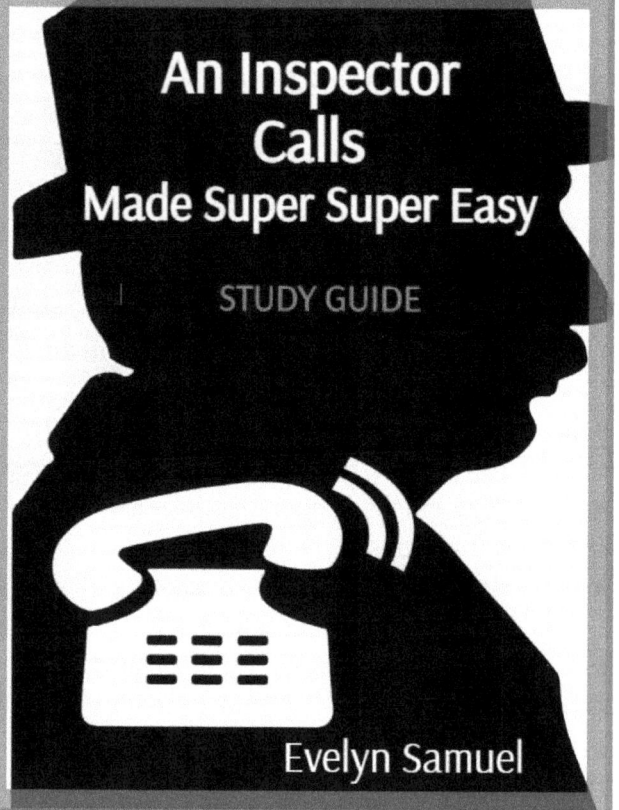

Evelyn Samuel

An Inspector Calls
Made Super Super Easy

STUDY GUIDE

Evelyn Samuel

Milton Keynes UK
Ingram Content Group UK Ltd.
UKHW052147200924
448623UK00011B/91

9 781739 998127